SANDEEP TREHAN
Weaving Values into Success

BLUEROSE PUBLISHERS
India | U.K.

Copyright © Sandeep Trehan 2025

All rights reserved by author. No part of this publication may be reproduced, stored in a retrieval system or transmitted in any form or by any means, electronic, mechanical, photocopying, recording or otherwise, without the prior permission of the author. Although every precaution has been taken to verify the accuracy of the information contained herein, the publisher assumes no responsibility for any errors or omissions. No liability is assumed for damages that may result from the use of information contained within.

BlueRose Publishers takes no responsibility for any damages, losses, or liabilities that may arise from the use or misuse of the information, products, or services provided in this publication.

For permissions requests or inquiries regarding this publication, please contact:

BLUEROSE PUBLISHERS
www.BlueRoseONE.com
info@bluerosepublishers.com
+91 8882 898 898
+4407342408967

ISBN: 978-93-6261-220-5

Typesetting: Pooja Sharma

First Edition: January 2025

Dedication

To my grandparents, for shaping my value system & foundation of my life

Late Shri Gopal Das Trehan & Late Smt Ram Rakhi Trehan

Synopsis

"Whistle of Hope: Weaving Values into Success" is an extraordinary book written by Sandeep Trehan. This captivating memoir offers readers a glimpse into author's transformative journey, shaped by his humble beginnings in a quaint town. Through vivid storytelling, author shares the invaluable wisdom he acquired while growing up, under the watchful guidance of his cherished grandfather.

This enchanting tale explores a myriad of themes, from the importance of embracing one's roots, to the power of resilience and determination. Drawing upon intimate anecdotes from his childhood, author reveals how the simplicity of village life enriched his character and instilled in him the values of hard work, integrity, and compassion. The book elaborates how these simple values can drive a person to be more innovative and technology driven to accomplish his dreams.

By intertwining captivating narratives with profound life lessons, the book takes readers on a thought-provoking journey. Author's experiences serve as a testament to the transformative impact of genuine human connections and the immense potential that lies within everyone.

Acknowledgements

Writing this book has been a beautiful experience, allowing me to relive my childhood, academic, and professional life. I sincerely thank my father for inspiring me to write this book. His teachings have been the foundation not only of my life but also of many events in this book.

Special thanks to my family members who have been part of my many learnings and successes and have always supported me in my various endeavors. I would like to acknowledge the support of all my friends who spent time discussing my life events and provided valuable support.

I am grateful to my colleagues, both current and from other organizations, who have helped with their input on the events to be included in this book.

Lastly, it has been a pleasure to work with BlueRose Publishers, and the cooperation of their staff is much appreciated.

Preface

I started my professional career in a family-owned private company on the shop floor as a production supervisor and then moved to Public Sector JV, a global multinational, the biggest private player, a family-owned small private company, and a company owned by a private equity fund. This multi-organizational experience from the last forty years and beyond has provided me with the opportunity to continue learning and managing change.

The joy of living can be experienced only when we follow our dreams. There is no measurement for dreams; only their fulfilment determines their greater value for you. As a young engineering student, I thought of digging the well and feeling the oil in my hand, and I did it with grace while working for a small oil company after leaving the job at the biggest private sector company. The feeling of fulfilment was immense. Similarly, while working on the small project on behalf of India Oil Corporation Ltd. in 1991 with GAIL to demonstrate CNG use in the transport sector, I got the aim of working for the use of cleaner fuels. This small stem has created a revolution in India, and presently, over 6,000 CNG stations are operating to supply CNG for over 6-7 million vehicles in India. The situation in 2018 also led me to be a co-founder of THINK Gas, which is now one of the leading private CGD players. These have been simple and ordinary achievements, but they make a big statement that if a deed is done right, it brings appreciation and earns recognition from the people you love.

I had a wonderful childhood in a joint family. My grandfather, Shri Gopal Das Trehan, was a retired postmaster of a small place in Kishangarh. He taught me simple things like lessons on kindness, care, simplicity, and good communication, which have always inspired me in life. The lessons of childhood are and can never be taught in any university. Your life should be a manifestation of doing the right thing. There should be no doubt that when doing the right and simple things, you are likely to face difficulties and challenges, but with discipline and determination, you can always make your life successful.

My father, Shri Om Prakash Trehan, has been my source of strength. He just laid down a few ground rules for life: discipline and spending within means. It worked very well for me. He always emphasized that we should know about our eco-system, know what is happening around us, and remain focused on our goals in life. I feel proud to say that he still tracks my work, my failures and successes, and continuously guides me to work harder and do better. It was he who advised me to write a book on various experiences from my life journey just three months ago.

I had always enjoyed communicating with our family members, friends, and colleagues. I did develop the habit of sharing a few examples of history and society while making a point in any discussion. It has worked very well in winning some good deals during my period as an employee. In 2008, when I used to share my car with my colleagues while travelling to the office, they suggested I write a book on my experiences, and I promised them to do so as and when I would get some accomplishments.

Everything and everyone in this world are connected, so it is important we keep doing the job we have in hand efficiently. I have a strong belief that whatever we are doing today has a correlation to the activity we will do in the future. Therefore, it is important that we do our present job efficiently and in the right way. I am writing this book to make the statement that "doing right things is more important than doing things efficiently." My young colleagues must weave their dreams; the first step is to think, then work hard and focus on doing the right things.

When I started writing this book, I got the opportunity to live through my childhood, my youth, my college, and my professional life again. I reached out to my childhood friends, school and college friends, and colleagues from earlier organizations for their valuable input. I could include in this book only major incidents, keeping the objective of this book in mind. It is quite possible that some of the incidents or events have been inadvertently not mentioned.

The book presents Kishangarh's boy, who comes from a joint family and started his life under the shadow of his grandparents in a free, natural environment. He has been blessed with a value system that was given to him by his parents, grandparents, and teachers, and with which, he dreams of achieving simple and innovative things. The book also shows his memorable relationships with his siblings, family members, friends, and their family members. The learnings, failures, and success stories of professional life have also been captured for the reader. The book narrates the beautiful, joyful journey in a humble way, saying that each individual creates his own ecosystem and energy system and plays a particular role in it. The foundation of life is hard work, focusing on the present task, and at the end, achievements are expressions of God's will. The book is written for young people who have been working in organizations—small or big, private or government. This is to express that designations have no long-term value; you only grow when you develop skills to lead challenges, take risks, and manage them successfully.

Growth has happened in the last 50 years, without or with the help of technology. Technology can only provide tools for either monitoring or accelerating events, but results are obtained with a positive attitude and the will to win. A strong, positive mind will always bring the best out of you. Being punctual is more important than having a smart watch. To respond to customers, being customer-focused is more important than having multiple communication tools and apps in the organization. A promise to deliver on time is more important than price, sales promotion, or product story

The book will inspire millions of young colleagues working in various organizations across India and abroad to write their own success stories.

Sandeep Trehan

Contents

1: A Humble Beginning.. 1

2: Cherishing the Joy of Simple Moments.. 6

3: The Scent of Desert 11

4: School Life: The Beginning... 15

5: Threads of Wisdom: Lessons from the Past and the
Classroom and its influence on my life 21

6: Moral Lessons: Guiding Life's Journey... 32

7: Shaping of a Young Mind 39

8: From Campus to Career: A Lifelong Journey of Growth 45

9: Milestones of Resilience and Collaboration.................................... 52

10: Guiding Lights: Life, Business, and Relationships...................... 60

11: Family Bonds and Personal Triumphs 70

12: Resilient Journeys of Professional and Personal Growth............ 81

13: Journey Into the Depths in Oil Exploration 87

14: The Rise of THINK Gas 104

15: The importance of Leadership in one's life............................... 122

16: Life's Driving Forces... 130

1: A Humble Beginning

Amidst simplicity, childhood lessons bloom, bridging past serenity with present enlightenment and nostalgia.

In the depths of the world where I live now, there are moments where I am taken back to my childhood. Living in the suburbs is indeed the magic of modernization, yet the allure of my early life pulls me away from the peace I often search for. Just being a simple boy from Kishangarh in Ajmer district in the Indian state of Rajasthan.

Kishangarh has memories of yesterday that made me who I am today. I belonged to a joint family where love, care, and togetherness were the three pillars of happiness. My childhood home has seen my birth and my early upbringing. The white walls of our family home have heard my first cry, as giving birth in hospitals wasn't a trend at that time.

Life was simple, yet its beauty at that moment cannot be compared to anything that I have experienced till now.

I used to live in a house that was surrounded by unique natural boundaries. While I could see Pond water touching the foundation of the house, the other end was facing a railway track at 200/250 m in the front. On one side, we had Pigeon Place, where hundreds of pigeons used to enjoy their food. It was a lovely blue sky at the top, which was revealing millions of stars in the night. The brightness of stars was filling the gap of no electricity in the house. I have never forgotten the game to track the various star formations in the night. My grandfather was a retired postmaster, and we were living in this house along with uncles and aunts.

Sometimes in my childhood, it used to start with the alarm clock of the train engine whistle. That whistle was the clock we needed to know that the sun had peeked through the sky. I got up from the embrace of my family and walked out to see the sun rising, the train passing by, and the serene view of the village on the other side of the pond.

No electricity and water supply were things that we never felt were a difficulty. Many times, after freshening up, my friend, Son of Landlord Milap Chand Verma, and I used to take a cow or two out for a round, and along the way, that one or two cows used to become a herd.

Rounding them all up without losing one, this particular memory taught me a few of the most important lessons of working with people: leadership, coordination, and communication.

Leading a herd is more than giving directions or shouting "hoiya"—it's like steering a ship through varied currents ~ it's understanding unspoken signals. Leading a team isn't just about talking but also about grasping what's not said. It's about clear communication and tuning into the team's silent cues. The effort was huge in the beginning, but in less than 3-4 days, we could see very disciplined cows walking straight in groups, like a perfect team.

This was fun when I was young, but as I grew up, it made me enlightened in a way that made me revisit each of my best memories to derive a lesson I could learn to be a better human.

Coming back home, after returning the cows to their families, I again rushed to the city library because newspapers weren't a daily occurrence, along with Grandfather after having breakfast.

Ah! A library, a sanctuary of stories nestled amidst the serene embrace of nature. It was a library maintained by the local town administration at less than 1 km once you crossed the railway station. Newspapers are spread on vertical stands, page by page, and it was fun to read them while standing. My grandfather used to guide me initially, but soon I developed an interest in sports and politics. Editorials were helpful in understanding key events of the day. I understand this library is still in operation, distributing a wealth of knowledge.

Upon entering, a comfortable silence envelope you—a sanctuary of knowledge and tales waiting to be discovered. Sunlight streams in through stained-glass windows, painting the worn wooden floors. The scent of aged parchment and whispers of wisdom hang in the air, a familiar fragrance that fills the soul with nostalgia.

Rows of bookshelves stand tall, embracing their worn and weathered companions. Each shelf tells its story—a history of countless readers who have turned these pages, leaving behind traces of their journeys within the dog-eared corners. Dust motes dance in the sunlight that filters through, casting a serene aura over the space.

The ambiance hums with soft murmurs—a few patrons engaged in whispered conversations, lost in worlds within pages. The librarian, a guardian of these treasures, moves with gentle grace, ever ready to guide and share the secrets held within the covers.

This was the library that was more than a temple of knowledge. It was my second home.

***

My childhood would be incomplete without recounting the joy I found in bathing at either the well or the nearby pond. Even now, the freshness of those times lingers within me, keeping the child in me alive. We'd pull water up in small buckets, always careful to tie the rope securely before lowering it—an early lesson in the importance of holding on to what matters. I remember watching how the rope, with each use, slowly ground away the stone edge of the well, leaving behind its quiet mark.

Bathing in the pond brought its own kind of wonder. The water reflected beautiful shades, shifting with the changing colors of the sky, a peaceful spectacle that felt almost magical.

The visits to the bageechi—the orchard—are memories I cherish deeply. The owner, a family friend, welcomed us, letting us freely pick and enjoy whatever fruits caught our fancy. I can still recall the taste of fresh blackberries, mulberries, and other fruits, each choice an expression of pure freedom. We had the liberty to select the color, flavor, and fruit we desired. Today, as life has shifted and grown more confined within professional boundaries, that sense of choice feels much more limited. The freedom to fully choose— to indulge in what truly brings joy—has been replaced by compromises, small but constant, in the course of growing up.

The Government Library in the Central Market, Kishangarh

Living without modern conveniences like electricity and water never felt like a hardship because it was filled with love, laughter, and life lessons.

"The humble beginnings in Kishangarh taught me the value of simplicity, connection to nature, and the strength of community. From herding cows to visiting the library, these experiences laid the foundation for leadership, perseverance, and the appreciation of life's unique pleasures."

2: Cherishing the Joy of Simple Moments

A reflection on how everyday experiences and simple acts shape our character, reminding us to find joy in life's smallest moments.

Nowadays, acts of service are looked at as a burden rather than providing someone with a sense of relief or comfort. My grandfather often used to ask me to fetch him a glass of water. Now, in that era, Aqua Guard/Refrigerator was a dream that we never even dreamed of, so I used to pick up one bucket and walk to the well to get some fresh water for him and my family to drink. And somehow, it used to be my utmost pleasure to do so.

As the days passed by, sometimes I used to sit with my grandmother and listen to her narrate the Ramayana and Mahabharata with so much faith and purity that it strengthened my beliefs too. Before the sun set, my family used to eat and get everything ready for the night, like cleaning the lamps and ensuring they lasted the entire night.

My birthplace and my home - Kishangarh

Often, I used to massage my grandfather's feet or fan him to sleep with a newspaper or a hand fan. There was no sleeping pattern. Sometimes I used to cuddle between my grandparents, while sometimes my siblings and I would sleep on the terrace while watching the clear night sky and the twinkling stars.

Sometimes while spending time at home, yet again with the fragrance of nature surrounding me, a sweet aroma of kheer filled the air. Ah! Dadaji ne kheer banai hai. I can go around the globe and eat all kinds of desserts, but the kheer he used to make is out of this universe. The perfect balance of sweetness and consistency of milk with the crunch of dry fruits in every bite.

Oh! The things I'd give up having just one bite again.

***

During my formative years, the sun-drenched afternoons unfolded a unique chapter of my education at my aunt's school, KD Jain Primary School. This unassuming institution, nestled within the embrace of familiarity, unknowingly laid the groundwork for my primary education. The school, a haven of learning and camaraderie, served as my haven during those languid afternoons. I didn't study in school but experienced the foundation of learning in my heart.

My aunt, a dedicated educator, became both my mentor and guide, weaving knowledge into the fabric of everyday moments. The classrooms echoed with the vibrant hum of curiosity, and the corridors whispered tales of countless lessons learned. The blackboard, adorned with chalk-drawn wisdom, held the keys to unlocking the mysteries of language and numbers.

As I immersed myself in the lively cadence of the school, each day became a new page in my educational journey. From scribbling the alphabet to unravelling the wonders of basic arithmetic, my afternoons were a canvas painted with the hues of discovery.

Looking back, those seemingly ordinary afternoons were the steppingstones that shaped my academic foundation. The school, with its nurturing environment and the guidance of my aunt, not only imparted knowledge but sowed the seeds of a lifelong love for learning. It was in those sunlit corridors that the roots of my educational journey found fertile ground, laying the groundwork for the years of discovery that lay ahead.

***

The pings of the phones and smartwatches to notify you what is happening in the world are nothing when I remember the walk to the chaurahya of Kishangarh. This spot isn't just a location; it's like the heart of our town, where stories blend with everyday life.

Paths made of old stones wind under big trees, making a shady canopy. In the evening, everything turns into a beautiful picture, mixing memories and what's happening now.

You can hear the distant sounds of the market mixing with kids' laughter as they play games on the steps. Smells of delicious street food fill the air, inviting everyone to try the tasty treats from the local vendors. It's like a lively melody where the stories of the past meet the busy sounds of today.

In the middle of all this, there's an old radio with a worn-out loudspeaker. We used to hear news of the day from All India Radio. This radio isn't just a machine; it's like a storyteller connecting everyone in town. As the sun goes down, the Chaurahya becomes a place where stories are shared. Life slows down, and the community enjoys the richness of these tales.

The Chaurahya isn't just a space; it's a reminder of the strong traditions in our town, even as the world changes. Here, the beeps of modern gadgets fade away, letting the timeless voices and stories take over, like whispers from the past meeting the present.

Fetching water, listening to my grandmother's stories, and sharing time with loved ones showed me that joy often comes from the smallest, most meaningful acts.

Kishangarh is now a developed town with a proposed airport and is famous for the marble market. The station is also now relocated a few kilometers away from the house.

"These experiences shaped my understanding of life, reminding me to cherish simplicity and the bonds that truly matter."

3: The Scent of Desert

Echoes of nature's symphony and tales

Sri Karanpur, situated in the Ganganagar District of Rajasthan, is a quaint town. It shares its northwest border with the neighbouring country, Pakistan.

I visited with my grandparents, and there's a mix of memories that feel like a special story. The place is kind of desert-like, with a few trains passing through and beautiful mornings. I remember the sand dunes not far away—being there felt like being at home in the desert, comforting and familiar. The canal and the desert were not far from my uncle's house. We used to have fun around the tube wells and enjoy the cold sand and the earthy smell after rain. The mornings were beautiful, with clear skies and stars fading away as night turned into day. But amid all the nice memories, there were also reminders of tough times during the war. People used to hide in bunkers for safety. It was a rare experience for a child like me—something most people today won't get to see. Karanpur holds these memories close, like secrets waiting to be remembered again.

In the small village of Karanpur, life was painted with the colours of simplicity. One of the cherished pastimes was bathing in the canal, a ritual that brought the community together, where laughter echoed against the gentle flow of water. Under the night sky, we found our own cosmic playground, searching for constellations and even dreaming of glimpsing a polar bear in those glittering stars. But now, it feels like that celestial magic has faded. The stars that once lit up the night have dimmed, lost behind the veils of modern life. The pure joy of being enveloped by nature's embrace seems distant in today's hurried world. In Karanpur, that connection to the natural environment was a treasure, a gift that seems elusive in the fast-paced present.

The dawn of each day in Sri Karanpur heralded a symphony of nature's awakening. Our mornings commenced with a ritualistic walk, an activity that seemed to harmonize perfectly with the tranquility of the desert landscape. The sensation of cool desert sand beneath my bare feet was a delightful dance between earth and soul, grounding me in the serenity of the moment.

The tube well, a cherished oasis in the arid expanse, became our post-walk sanctuary. The refreshing embrace of its water washed away the traces of the desert journey, leaving us revitalized and ready for the day's adventures. The simple joy of bathing after a walk became a ritual that transcended the physical, cleansing not just the body but also the spirit.

Yet, life in the desert held its surprises, and one of them came in the form of the occasional desert storm. The winds would whip up the fine sand into a frenzy, creating an ethereal dance of particles that painted the air in shades of gold. Amidst the swirling chaos, we learned to navigate the gusts, shielding ourselves from the elements. It was in those moments of nature's fury that we found a different kind of exhilaration, a communion with the untamed spirit of the desert.

Sri Karanpur was not just a canvas of serene landscapes but also an arena where nature and adventure coexisted. A short journey to the nearby canal became a thrilling escapade, offering the allure of a cool swim and the enchantment of a nearby rose garden. The canal, a lifeline in the desert, mirrored the contrast between the arid surroundings and the oasis it provided. Immersing ourselves in its waters was a baptism into nature's bounty, a stark contrast to the dry expanse that surrounded us.

Living in a border area meant living with the echoes of history, and Sri Karanpur had witnessed its share of armed action in 1965. As a testament to the resilience of its inhabitants, the locals dug their own bunkers of the Z type during those tumultuous times. These bunkers, now silent witnesses to the passage of time, stood as monuments to the strength and unity that defined the community.

Amidst these historical echoes, my childhood unfolded with unique experiences, one of which included travelling on a goods train. My uncle's association with the Indian Railways granted us this extraordinary opportunity. Chewing on sugar cane as we rode along the tracks, the rhythmic clatter of the wheels became a lullaby, serenading us on this unconventional journey. The landscape passing by was a tapestry of fields and villages, each telling its own story, etching memories that would endure.

> The joy of simple things, like laughing with family or enjoying nature's beauty, is what really matters.

From those memories, I learned something important.

Sri Karanpur was a place where the ordinary became extraordinary, where the routine was infused with the magic of the desert. In the heart of those memories, Sri Karanpur remains a cherished chapter, a testament to the richness that can be found in the simplicity of life and the vast expanse of the desert horizon.

"Freedom of having pleasant childhood options we had in Sri Karanpur, was marked by simple joys—playing under the stars, swimming in the canal, and connecting with nature. These experiences taught me that true happiness often comes from the freedom to explore, laugh, and immerse oneself in life's purest moments."

4: School Life: The Beginning

Lessons carved in humble corridors, friendships bloom, and life blossoms.

In the sandook (box) of my vibrant memories of my childhood, the Railway School in Ganpati Nagar, Jaipur, emerges as a beacon of education that transcended the limitations of infrastructure, creating an environment rich in values and life lessons. The humble yet dedicated teachers, not affluent in worldly riches but abundant in wisdom, imparted not just academic knowledge but also the principles that shaped character and family values.

The journey to school was a daily adventure, crossing the bustling station with my siblings. Along the way, a quaint toy shop owner captured our youthful imaginations, unveiling the magic of new toys with a warmth that transcended commercial transactions. Little did I know that this simple act of generosity would resonate years later when, as a parent wanting to buy a toy for my son, the same shop owner refused payment, embodying the enduring affection that binds communities.

A literary journey intertwined with the railroad tracks became a ritual as I borrowed books from the iconic AH Wheeler shop. Nandan, Parang, and Sports Week were portals to different worlds, and sharing this literary exploration with my friend Prakash and his sister added a layer of camaraderie to the experience. It was the early time of my life when we learned a few lessons about cricket from Prakash. We used to wait in the evening for him so that he could come with a cricket kit, and we could all play.

The daily walk on the railway track was more than a shortcut; it was a balancing act that added a touch of excitement to mundane routines. Completing homework ahead of schedule became a way to help friends, fostering a culture of collaborative learning and mutual support within the school community.

During school intervals, the railway line beckoned us to explore the adjacent farms. For a meagre sum of Rs 0.05, the farmer/owner generously allowed us to revel in the simple joys of plucking tomatoes, carrots, radishes, and other farm delights. This rustic interaction with agriculture not only provided a delicious diversion but also instilled a sense of appreciation for the hard work of those tilling the land.

The school itself, lacking in conventional infrastructure, became a canvas for unconventional learning. Some classes unfolded beneath the comforting shade of trees in an open-air classroom where the lessons of life mingled with academic teachings. This unique setting opened the door to another dimension—the world of club cricket matches. Legends like Salim Durrani graced these matches, their cricketing prowess captivating the young hearts on the sidelines. It was during these matches that my fascination with cricket blossomed, sparked by the charismatic Salim Durrani, whose heroics on overseas tours and the famous six on demand became etched in my cricket-loving heart.

School life extended beyond the classroom, and my friend Prakash's possession of a cricket kit brought us together daily for spirited cricket sessions. This nucleus of friendship expanded, weaving a network of camaraderie that mirrored the diverse tapestry of our experiences.

If one is in Jaipur, he cannot be untouched by the joy of kite flying. Kite flying added another layer to our shared adventures. As a supporting player in the kite-flying sessions, I witnessed the thrill of battles in the sky, each cut string symbolizing a victory in the ephemeral world of kites. The laughter, the camaraderie, and the shared triumphs in these simple pleasures created memories that echo through the corridors of time. Flying a kite with Prakash was an experience, as was flying with Piyush at his house in the central city. At each Makar Sankranti on January 14, one can see blue being approached by colourful kites. Kite is a symbol of life where Kite has to be going high either along or against the wind direction. Kite flying became another cherished pursuit, especially during the vibrant festival of Makar Sankranti every 14th January. The skies adorned with colorful kites and the thrill of maneuvering the string created an annual spectacle that brought joy and camaraderie to the community.

The Railway School in Ganpati Nagar, Jaipur, was more than an institution of learning; it was a crucible of experiences that shaped values, friendships, and a lifelong love for the simple joys of life. Its unconventional charm and the extraordinary teachers who nurtured young minds transcended the constraints of brick and mortar, leaving an indelible mark on the hearts of those fortunate enough to walk its humble corridors. I studied at this school until I completed my 8th standard in 1973. I always remember the face of one of the primary school teachers, Mr. Devendra Singh, who used to come to school by bicycle and taught the best lessons of life in a very humble way. His advice to focus on whatever activity you do and give your best is very fundamental but has not been forgotten. He always encouraged students to share their knowledge with fellow students and everyone else to become better.

I was also a scout in the school, which helped me learn some skills and build confidence to become a better citizen.

***

I was ten years old, and being the eldest son, I had a responsibility to write to all our relatives during the first week of every month. I used to go to the post office and purchase post cards and inland letters... At that time, most of the families did not have land lines, and having a phone at home was a luxury. Postal communication used to be the best solution. I used to send these letters about our well-being and other related activities. We used to get replies by the third or fourth week. Any missing reply was cause for concern. The third week used to be very interesting because we used to wait for the postman to deliver letters to our house. It was a typical sentence from us in the evening: Did we receive any letters? It was fun. Everyone used to go through the letters.

During my professional days, I also used to maintain a diary with addresses and phone numbers so that if I ever visited the place or city of a friend or relative, I would make sure to find some time to meet them. This has helped to create good bonding among family members as well as some of my friends.

Now we have progressed in technology, and each one of us has a telephone, smart phone, or email. There are various ways to connect people every day and every minute through apps. We can send written messages and pictures 24x7 across the world. But unfortunately, the willingness to communicate has decreased. No one inquires whether any letter or message has come. The simple schedule of writing and receiving letters once a month has been replaced by technologically advanced tools and methods.

It is important that we communicate. We must understand that the will to communicate only provides us with ways to build bridges.

In a world increasingly driven by technology, the essence of meaningful communication and personal connections remains invaluable.

"From the warmth of a humble toy shop owner to the life lessons learned from dedicated teachers and the joy of handwritten letters, it underscores how these seemingly ordinary moments have shaped my values and relationships. It reminds us to cherish and uphold the timeless virtues of community, friendship, and heartfelt exchange, which continue to enrich our lives despite the rapid pace of modern advancements."

The Railway School in Ganpati Nagar, Jaipur

The cricket ground near my school

The charismatic Salim Durrani

5: Threads of Wisdom and its influence

Family, friends, and teachers weave enduring lessons into our lives, shaping our character and guiding us with their wisdom...

When I delved deeper into the mosaic of my childhood, the Vyas family and the Wadhawa family were vibrant threads, weaving tales of warmth, wisdom, and enduring connections. Mr. Om Dutt Vyas, an esteemed colleague of my father, became a fixture in my young life. His home was a sanctuary of positivity; he always kept cows at home, and I always had the opportunity to have buttermilk during my visit, where his blessings echoed promises of a future adorned with prosperity and joy. His genuine love and well-wishes left an indelible mark, a beacon guiding me towards the aspirations he envisioned. I also became friendly with his children, and we are still in touch.

The Wadhawa family, another chapter in this narrative, welcomed me with open arms. I used to have a cup of tea with Aunty and have discussions with Uncle on various national subjects, even if Bitto was either sleeping or busy. Bitto, a dear friend from their household, embarked on a noble journey to become a doctor, driven by a profound dedication to caring for his mother. His commitment to his profession and his infectious warmth has endured through the years, and we remain connected, a testament to the enduring bonds formed during those formative days. Bitto is now Dr. Sunil Wadhwa, a renowned cardiologist managing his clinic in Lajpat Nagar, New Delhi.

***

In my memories, there's a simple yet profound moment etched—a lesson learned while buying moong lentils from the local market. It was a lesson on the importance of never being in debt, a financial philosophy imparted by my father: always spend within the resources one has. It all began when my father handed me a small sum of money, Rs 0.25, and asked me to purchase 250 grams of Moong ki dal from our neighbourhood grocery shop.

Upon reaching the shop, I approached the shopkeeper, a friendly and familiar face in our small community. I requested 250 grams of dal and watched as he skilfully weighed the lentils and poured them into a small paper bag. I asked the shopkeeper for the cost, and as he recited the amount, reality dawned upon me. I had fallen short by a mere 5 paise. The rate had gone up from Rs 1 per kg to Rs 1.20 per kg.

The shopkeeper told me that I could return Rs 0.05 later. On reaching home, I narrated the incident of being short by Rs 0.05 to my father. Instead of acknowledging my effort, he scolded me sternly, his voice tinged with disappointment. "If you were short of 5 paise," he chided, "you could have bought 200 grams of dal instead of 250." What compelled you to be in debt to the shopkeeper?" He immediately sent me back in the hot summer to return Rs 0.05 to the shopkeeper.

Those words, simple yet profound, held the crux of the lesson my father aimed to teach me. They were more than just a scolding; they were a revelation. My young mind began to grasp the concept - the idea that borrowing, no matter how small the amount, could be avoided with prudent choices and living within one's means.

Today, as I navigate the complex world of finances, I carry that lesson with me. I am reminded of my father's words every time I make a financial decision. I've learned to manage my expenses judiciously and, when necessary, make choices within my budget to avoid the burden of debt. In a world where borrowing has become a norm, and credit is readily available, the lesson of living within my means and never being in debt has served as a guiding principle. It has shielded me from the pitfalls of excessive financial commitments and allowed me to lead a life of fiscal prudence.

> It is a legacy that I, in turn, hope to pass on to the generations that follow, ensuring that the wisdom of never being in debt continues to resonate through the ages.

As I look back on that day, I am grateful for the valuable lesson my father taught me, a lesson that has echoed through the corridors of time and remains an integral part of my financial philosophy.

***

Studying on the rooftop under the shade of a Neem tree was a cherished routine. The natural canopy created by the tree offered a serene environment, where the melodious chirping of parrots and the majestic presence of peacocks added a touch of magic to the learning process. The positive energy emanating from this unconventional classroom fueled a love for knowledge that transcended the boundaries of traditional study spaces.

Summer also brought an annual tradition: receiving sweaters from maternal aunts. Despite the physical distance, their ability to visualize and send perfectly sized sweaters bespoke a deep familial connection. These annual gifts carried not just warmth but also a sense of love that transcended the tangible. I frequently spent my vacations at my aunt's places in Agra and Kanpur. These trips were more than just getaways; they were opportunities to bask in the warmth of family gatherings and immerse myself in the cultural tapestry of these diverse locations. Agra, rich with historical charm, and Kanpur, vibrant and lively, offered me not only leisure but also a profound connection to my roots. These visits created lasting memories, each contributing to the tapestry of my personal experiences.

Embedded in the golden rules set by my parents was the directive to return home after play, ensuring I stepped through the door before sunset or 7 p.m., whichever came earlier. This seemingly simple rule was a testament to the care and concern that defined the nurturing environment of my childhood. It instilled a sense of responsibility and discipline that would become foundational in shaping my character.

The specter of the 1971 war loomed large in my childhood memories. A trip to the station revealed the gravity of the situation as trains ferried tanks and arms and wounded soldiers returned, bearing the scars of conflict. It was a sobering lesson about the harsh realities of war, a stark contrast to the innocence of childhood play.

The transition from traditional cooking methods, using cow dung and wood, to modern conveniences like kerosene stoves and eventually LPG marked a significant change in household dynamics. Convincing the family to embrace these technological shifts was no small feat, illustrating the challenges that accompany ushering in change. The journey from Angeethi to LPG was not just a shift in cooking methods but a microcosm of the broader societal evolution during those transformative years. It was difficult to convince my grandmother to eat chapati cooked from LPG rather than Angeethi. Right and simple communication becomes important for any transition.

I also learned a great lesson about the value of money in life during my summer vacation at my maternal grandfather's house. He lost a 25-paisa coin under the bed while changing clothes. He made the massive bed removed to recover 25 paisa coins. His statement was that it is very difficult, and you must work hard to earn money, so it is important we respect our hard work and value money. A very simple but important lesson.

As I reflect on these fragments of my childhood, I see a mosaic painted with the colours of connection, wisdom, and the resilience required to navigate change. The lessons learned in those formative years continue to shape my perspective, serving as a compass guiding me through the complexities of adulthood.

***

The corridors of Mahavir School, spanning the years 1973 to 1976, echo with the resonance of transformative experiences and enduring lessons. The imprint of dedicated educators, the camaraderie of new friendships, and the pursuit of passions collectively defined this chapter of my academic journey.

Mr. Jhalani, an embodiment of patience and commitment, stands out as the architect of my mathematical understanding. His willingness to extend extra time and effort to ensure his students grasp the intricacies of mathematics left an indelible mark. It was not merely about numbers and formulas; rather, it was his commitment to impart knowledge and fostering love for the subject that set Mr. Jhalani apart. His dedication laid the foundation for a lifelong appreciation of the beauty inherent in mathematical concepts.

Post-retirement, the baton of mathematical enlightenment passed to Dr. Tej Karan Dandia. His "Art of Mathematics" sessions were more than lessons; they were an exploration of the subject's aesthetic nuances. Dr. Tej Karan Dandia's unconventional approach breathed life into the equations, making mathematics not just a requirement but a canvas for creativity.

In the realm of literature and the Hindi language, Dr. Savitri Parmar emerged as a guiding light. Her approach went beyond rote memorization; she delved into the stories, unravelling the language, emotions, and purpose within. Dr. Parmar's classes were not just about textbooks; they were a gateway to understanding the profound layers of narrative and the nuanced use of language.

Life's unexpected turns, like an accident on my bicycle, revealed the true essence of the Mahavir School community. S. P. Jain, a teacher whose concern extended beyond the academic realm, played a pivotal role during this challenging time. His genuine care and support were not just a testament to the teacher-student relationship but a reflection of the nurturing environment that Mahavir School embodied.

Yet, amidst the pursuit of knowledge, the mischievous spirit of youth found expression in escapades like sneaking out through the window to catch a glimpse of the cricket team in action at X Vier School. The thrill of such escapades added a dash of spontaneity to the structured school routine.

New friendships emerged as a source of joy and solace. Piyush, with his simplicity, affection, and caring nature, became a pillar of support. The bonds forged during those school years transcended the classroom, enriching the saga of life with shared memories and enduring connections.

As the journey through Mahavir School progressed, the pivotal year of the XI standard marked a significant milestone. A daring drive to secure admission to an engineering college encapsulated the determination and ambition that were beginning to define my path forward.

The love for table tennis became a passion that spilled beyond the confines of the school. From playing in the school's interval to finding spaces at the GPO, Telephone Exchange, and eventually the SMS Stadium, the journey mirrored the expanding horizons of interests and pursuits.

In the delicate balance between play and study, the echoes of parental expectations reverberated. The late hours at home faced the inescapable questioning from my father, forcing a choice between play and studies. Under these circumstances, education and studies assumed paramount importance, shaping priorities and instilling a sense of discipline that would prove invaluable in the years to come.

Anuj Mathur, a formidable figure leading the annual parade, later retired from the army as a Major General. Although my personal inclination didn't align with my love for parades, I vividly recall being a part of that spectacle, an experience that, in retrospect, held a unique charm. Anuj Mathur's leadership conveyed a sense of discipline and dedication, traits that would later find their place in the mosaic of my own character.

Amidst the structured routines of school life, a delightful hobby emerged: the collection of postal stamps. This pursuit opened windows to the world, introducing me to countries, their leaders, landmark buildings, and significant events. The first-day cover collection from the General Post Office (GPO) became a treasure trove of knowledge, fostering a curiosity about the diverse cultures and histories encapsulated in those tiny, colourful squares.

In the tapestry of friendships, the Piyush family added a thread of simplicity and spirituality. Bhai Sahib, Piyush's elder brother, radiated positivity, shaping our discussions around movies into meaningful reflections on purpose and significance. Conversations about films like "Anand" and "Bawarchi" transcended casual chatter, becoming avenues for philosophical exploration. The simple gestures of the tenant's daughter, offering tea during visits, became poignant moments etched in the heart.

The Ranbir family, with whom I shared bicycle rides to school, introduced me to the beauty of poetry through the diary filled with shayaris that adorned their house. Cricket matches at their home, complete with the inevitable breaking of bottles in jute bags, became a cherished ritual. Ranbir's brother, a wonderful person, continues to be a steadfast friend, a testament to the enduring bonds formed during those carefree days.

Vivek's family was a haven of studiousness and warmth. Vivek's academic prowess, often topping the class, reflected the scholarly environment nurtured by his father, a professor in history at the University of Rajasthan. Spending time with the family was not just an opportunity for intellectual enrichment but also a culinary delight, as he savoured the delicious meals crafted by his mother.

The Tandon family was more than just classmates; we evolved into a closely-knit group that journeyed through school and engineering college together. Our bond strengthened as we studied in the newly constructed house, amidst the background score of music. This period marked the genesis of my love for songs, a passion that continues to resonate in my life. The Tandons' appreciation for art and culture, especially Kathak programmes, left an enduring impression, shaping our collective taste and pursuits.

In the supportive backdrop of board exams, D.K. Tiwari, a gentleman with a generous heart, provided me with a space to study. His kindness and encouragement played a pivotal role in my academic progress. A stalwart in the Commercial Department of Western Railway, his frequent travels did nothing to diminish his commitment to fostering my growth.

As I reflect on these memories, I am reminded that the memories, i.e. the lessons of my life are filled not just with personal achievements but also with colourful memories of relationships and shared moments. Each family mentioned here, each friend, and each mentor contributed to the canvas of my formative years, leaving an enduring legacy of warmth, wisdom, and shared experiences. These threads continue to intertwine with the fabric of my present, a testament to the profound impact of those cherished days.

School life has allowed me to enrich my knowledge and skills in Hindi and Sanskrit. A few of the poems, as explained by teachers, have become part of life. Mahavir School, with its dedicated educators, supportive community, and kaleidoscope of experiences, was more than an institution of learning. It was a crucible of character, an arena where academic pursuits, friendships, and personal growth converged. The lessons I imbibed during those transformative years continue to shape my journey, a testament to the enduring impact of a school that went beyond textbooks and classrooms to sculpt individuals ready to navigate the complexities of life.

"The influence of family, friends, and teachers weaves a rich tapestry of life lessons and enduring wisdom. As we navigate our youth and beyond, the guidance and connections from these pivotal figures shape our character and aspirations. Their lessons echo through our lives, leaving a lasting legacy that continues to guide and inspire us."

Mahivir School Teachers

Group picture of our respected teachers from Mahavir School. We can see Sh. MK Jain (4th from left) and Sh. G L Jhalani (5th from the left)

Our Respectful Dr Tej Karan Dandia

"Guru Govind dou khade, kake lagu paaye
Balihari Guru aapno, Govind diyo bataye"

"गुरु गोविंद दोऊ खड़े, काके लागूं पाय

बलिहारी गुरु आपनो, गोविंद दियो बताय"

6: Moral Lessons: Guiding Life's Journey

Importance of moral science and humanitarian subjects to nurture empathy, integrity, and compassion.

During my studies in mathematics and science, immersed in the world of equations and materials, it was the resonance of short stories and Sanskrit that lingered in my heart. Amidst the complexity of equations and scientific instruments, it became evident that human emotions and narratives held a profound significance. These stories and the beauty of Sanskrit illuminated the path, emphasizing the profound truth that our humanity and connections transcend the tangible, enriching us as compassionate individuals.

In the realm of literature, poetry holds a unique place—a sanctuary where emotions, thoughts, and the beauty of language converge to create a tapestry of profound expression. Among the myriad verses that have touched my soul, three stand out as beacons of poetic brilliance—Makhan Lal Chaturvedi's "Phoolo ki Abhilasha," Subhadra Kumari Chauhan's "Khoob ladi Mardani who to Jhansi wali Rani Thi," and the timeless verses of Ghalib.

"Phoolo ki Abhilasha" by Makhan Lal Chaturvedi is a poetic marvel that has resonated with generations. The title translates to "The Aspiration of Flowers," and in its verses, one finds an ode to the unquenchable yearning for freedom, growth, and fulfillment. Chaturvedi's evocative words paint a vivid picture of flowers aspiring to bloom, a metaphor for the indomitable human spirit seeking to reach its full potential despite adversities. The poem encapsulates the essence of hope, resilience, and the relentless pursuit of one's dreams—a timeless anthem that continues to inspire.

> मुझे तोड़ लेना बनमाली,
> उस पथ पर देना तुम फेंक
> मातृ-भूमि पर शीश-चढ़ाने,
> जिस पथ पर जावें वीर अनेक

"Khoob ladi Mardani who to Jhansi wali Rani Thi" by Subhadra Kumari Chauhan immortalizes the valor and strength of Rani Lakshmibai of Jhansi. These verses are not just lines on paper but a spirited anthem that reverberates with echoes of bravery. Chauhan, through her poetic prowess, captures the essence of the fearless queen who fought valiantly against the forces of oppression. The poem transcends its historical context, becoming a testament to the power of women and their unwavering resolve in the face of adversity. It's a literary gem that pays homage to the indelible mark left by Rani Lakshmibai on the pages of history.

> सिंहासन हिल उठे राजवंशों ने भृकुटी तानी थी
> बूढ़े भारत में भी आई फिर से नयी जवानी थी
> गुमी हुई आज़ादी की कीमत सबने पहचानी थी
> दूर फिरंगी को करने की सबने मन में ठानी थी
>
> चमक उठी सन सत्तावन में, वह तलवार पुरानी थी
> बुंदेले हरबोलों के मुँह हमने सुनी कहानी थी
> खूब लड़ी मर्दानी वह तो झाँसी वाली रानी थी

Mirza Ghalib, a luminary in Urdu and Persian poetry, crafted verses that have withstood the test of time. His ghazals and philosophical musings delve into the complexities of life, love, and human experience. Ghalib's poetry is a delicate dance of words, where each verse is a brushstroke on the canvas of emotions. His exploration of pain, love, and the existential question of existence resonates across generations. "Dil-e-Nadan Tujhe Hua Kya Hai" and "Hazaron Khwahishen Aisi" are poignant expressions of the human heart's intricacies, showcasing Ghalib's mastery in weaving together the threads of profound contemplation.

These poets, each unique in style and thematic resonance, have left an indelible mark on my literary journey. The verses I hold dear are not just words on paper; they are windows into the human soul, invitations to explore the depths of emotions and intellect. As I reflect on the impact of these poems, I find that they have become companions in moments of solitude, offering solace, inspiration, and a profound connection to the shared human experience.

Makhan Lal Chaturvedi's celebration of aspiration, Subhadra Kumari Chauhan's tribute to courage, and Ghalib's exploration of the human psyche—all intertwine to create a symphony of poetic brilliance. Each poet has become a guide, a confidant, and a source of introspection. The beauty of poetry lies in its ability to transcend time, bridging gaps between individuals, cultures, and eras. These verses, like timeless melodies, continue to echo in the corridors of my mind, offering a refuge in moments of contemplation and a celebration in moments of joy.

"Bade Bhaisaab" is a short story written by the renowned Hindi-Urdu writer, Munshi Premchand. It delves into the complexities of familial relationships and the impact of social status on individual lives.

> *We learn that a man is not big due to his age but due to his work and duties.*

The story outlines how an elder brother acts responsibly and takes care of his younger brother, he owns his responsibility more than his age and always ensure that his younger brother makes his future.

The experiences should be recognized and valued. Today we are progressing but forgetting the basic values. We shall also value experience in life as many of us. May not be highly educated, like mother but she knows what is good for her child and how they should be brought up and be successful in life. Sometimes experience has a value which cannot be compensated by higher education.

Adding on there are two shlokas very close to my heart which means: -

"शैले शैले न माणिक्य मौक्तिकं न गजे गजे।

साधवो न हि सर्वत्र चन्दनं न वने वने ॥

Translation in Hindi:

"न प्रत्येक पर्वत पर मणि-माणिक्य ही प्राप्त होते हैं न प्रत्येक हाथी के मस्तक से मुक्ता-मणि प्राप्त होती है। संसार में मनुष्यों की कमी न होने पर भी साधु पुरुष नहीं मिलते। इसी प्रकार सभी वनों में चन्दन के वृक्ष उपलब्ध नही होते। "

Translation in English:

"All the mountains do not have the precious stones, you will not get pearls from all the elephants; Noblemen cannot be found everywhere, sandalwood is not found in all the woods. (The good things are uncommon)."

"Vidya dadhati viniyam ": This shloka underscores the idea that true education not only imparts knowledge but also instills humility and compassion in individuals. It suggests that a student should not only seek knowledge for personal gain but also use it for the betterment of society and humanity. In English, it could be translated as "Knowledge is like a donor, it bestows humility."

"विद्या ददाति विनयं विनयाद् याति पात्रताम्।
पात्रत्वात् धनमाप्नोति धनाद् धर्म ततः सुखम्॥"

Translation in Hindi:

"शिक्षा से विनम्रता आती है, विनम्रता से व्यक्ति योग्य बनता है, योग्यता से धन प्राप्त होता है, और धन से धर्म का पालन होता है, जिससे अंततः सुख की प्राप्ति होती है।

Translation in English:

"Education imparts humility, humility leads to worthiness. Worthiness results in wealth, and from wealth one gains righteousness. From righteousness comes happiness."

Both shlokas reflect the themes of perseverance, humility, and the deeper purpose of education beyond mere academic achievement. Munshi Dhanpat Rai, inspired by these teachings, learns to apply these principles in his own life, striving for personal growth and moral development. The pinnacle of academic recognition arrived in the form of a scholarship bestowed upon me during the Xth standard. Beyond the financial support, this accolade became a cornerstone in shaping my belief in my abilities. The recognition fueled a sense of purpose and instilled confidence, setting the stage for a trajectory that transcended the walls of the classroom.

In the world of literature, these poets have woven threads of beauty, wisdom, and emotional resonance. Their verses are not mere compositions; they are gateways to a world where language transcends its utilitarian purpose, becoming a vessel for the profound and the sublime. As I navigate the literary landscapes shaped by these poets, I find myself enriched, enlightened, and forever captivated by the enduring magic of their words.

Human emotions hold greater value than actions; being a good human being is paramount. I recall profound lines from renowned poets that have shaped my values and interactions with others. I am grateful to teachers who have adeptly elucidated the essence of these poems and shlokas, ensuring they are deeply understood and remembered throughout life.

"The true education goes beyond academic knowledge, instilling values of humility, compassion, and perseverance. The profound wisdom found in literature, poetry, and ancient teachings emphasizes the importance of human connections, emotional depth, and moral integrity. It teaches that success is not just measured by material achievements but by how we honour our responsibilities, respect experience, and nurture the soul with understanding and empathy."

7: Shaping of a Young Mind

In the corridors of academia, wisdom blooms, shaping futures with lessons learned, and friendships forged.

The journey through MREC, now MNIT, (Malviya National Institute of Technology, Jaipur) from 1976 to 1981 unfolded as a significant chapter in my life, marked by challenges, camaraderie, and a dynamic political landscape.

Admission to this prestigious college hinged primarily on performance in 11th standard, particularly in science subjects. A significant 50% of the student body hailed from other states, fostering a diverse environment. The transition from school to college was marked by an impressive feat, as almost 75% of our class secured admission in various engineering branches.

Ragging, an unavoidable initiation ritual, added a unique flavor to our college initiation. Dressed in white clothes with short hair, navigating through the challenges became a shared adventure. Surprisingly, it evolved beyond a mere ritual, fostering stronger bonds with seniors who provided invaluable support, guidance, and even study materials throughout our college tenure.

Language became a bridge and a barrier in our academic journey. With instructions and teachings delivered in English, the transition was a significant challenge, especially for those of us who had received education in Hindi until the 11th standard. Dictionaries became our constant companions as we grappled with textbooks written in a language foreign to our academic upbringing. The guidance from teachers and parents to maintain focus on sincere practice was very helpful.

The collaborative spirit of our class was evident in our approach to project work. If a peer struggled to complete their project, the collective response was simple: either help them finish it or collectively decide not to submit. This ethos of mutual support and shared responsibility characterized our academic pursuits. Additionally, we found joy in gathering for a cup of tea among four students. We cherished the anticipation of waiting for the postman to deliver the money order or eagerly awaiting a trunk call to connect with family members.

A memorable episode was the Golmaal movie escapade, where we collectively communicated to our Head of Department (HOD) that due to "unavoidable circumstances," we couldn't attend class and instead went to watch the movie. But the HOD caught us in the cinema hall during the interval as he himself came to watch the movie. This was similar to one of the scenes in the film GOLMAL, which we were watching. We expected the HOD to reprimand us the following day. In a surprising turn of events, the HOD responded with humor, suggesting that next time we plan such an outing, we should consider booking two extra tickets. This simple, good gesture earned him lots of respect from the students, and never again did we miss his class.

The college environment was not just academically charged but also politically sensitive, given that we entered college just after the emergency period. Strikes and protests became part of our college experience, and we actively participated in movements aimed at bringing about a change of government in 1977.

An industrial trip to Delhi IIT provided a glimpse into the world of computers, a technology that was yet to permeate our engineering curriculum. It was an era where we pursued engineering without the aid of the digital tools that are now integral to the field.

In honour of Professor Advani, students organized the Advani Memorial Basketball Tournament, a testament to the impact he had on our college community. This event not only celebrated the sporting spirit but also paid homage to a revered figure in our academic journey.

My academic pursuits were soon intertwined with real-world events, inspiring a project on oil and gas exploration on land. The backdrop of the Iran-Iraq war and the changing dynamics of the oil industry, coupled with the fall of the Shah of Iran, fueled a sense of urgency and relevance in exploring this critical aspect of the energy sector.

The aftermath of the war led to a surge in oil prices, underscoring the strategic importance of oil exploration. Determined to contribute to this field, I undertook the ambitious goal of discovering oil during my lifetime. This quest led me to countless libraries, where I meticulously gathered information to compile a comprehensive report on land-based oil and gas exploration. Typing the report with a single finger and manually preparing colored graphs, this endeavor became a labor of love, fueled by a genuine passion for the subject.

Sanjeev Agarwal, a college friend of mine, assisted me in preparing this report. With a typewriter at his disposal, we collaborated to type the entire document. During this time, coloured photocopying was not available, so we had to manually create maps and mark locations using coloured pens.

In this academic pursuit, the workshop instructors and technical assistants played a pivotal role. Their friendly demeanour and enthusiasm for imparting knowledge left an indelible mark. Their guidance extended beyond the curriculum, instilling in us a love for learning and an appreciation for the practical applications of our studies.

A special day in college changed my life. Professor Dr. Srinivasan shared important lessons for those about to step into public life. His words, full of wisdom, went beyond the classroom, leaving a lasting impression on my journey and career.

He talked about the dangers of giving in to peer pressure, especially when it comes to habits and choices. Professor Srinivasan, a former chain smoker, began by saying, "This is the first cigarette that shouldn't be smoked," sharing the difficulty of breaking a habit and warning against trying new things just because of societal pressure.

He suggested a practical strategy to resist such pressures: politely excuse yourself during repeated requests. This simple but effective technique has stayed with me, helping in situations where saying no was crucial.

> *Good company protects your values and keeps you out of compromising situations.*

The professor stressed the importance of being in good company. "Always be in good company," he said. While it was not a new idea, his words made it a guiding principle in my life. The reason was clear: This advice guided me through many decisions where sticking to my values was important.

When talking about public life, Professor Srinivasan highlighted the irreversible nature of our choices. These choices, he said, should shape our professional identity. Hard work, managing time well, being ethical, and telling the truth, according to him, were the key elements of a successful professional life.

Thinking about his words, I find them more relevant than ever. The world would be a better place if we embraced and practiced these principles in our daily lives. Professor Srinivasan's wise words are now a part of my personal philosophy and a reminder of how a mentor can shape one's character and choices.

Education fosters humility and collaboration, while strong ethical principles and wise guidance from mentors like Professor Srinivasan equip one to navigate both personal and professional challenges. "**Surrounding** oneself with good company, resisting negative peer pressure, and upholding integrity are essential to leading a meaningful and successful life."

Names left to right Dr R S Saxena, Dr V Srinivasan, Dr Rajan, Dr N Tanwani.

B.E Mechanical 1976 batch of MREC (MNIT Jaipur) who passed out in 1981-82

8: From Campus to Career: A Lifelong Journey of Growth

Echoes of camaraderie and shared moments weave a timeless narrative of growth.

As a day scholar, I had the opportunity to witness the unique and interesting dynamics of hostel life. The camaraderie among students, the anticipation of postman-delivered money, the shared meals in the hostel mess, and the camaraderie of students borrowing money wherever the postman made his deliveries—all these elements contributed to the rich tapestry of hostel life. Trunk calls, movie outings, and shared cups of tea created a sense of community that is hard to replicate in today's digital age.

The practical industrial training at esteemed institutions such as HMT Ajmer, NEI Jaipur, and on-the-job training with Kirloskar tractors marked pivotal moments in my academic journey. These experiences provided a bridge between theory and practice, allowing me to apply classroom knowledge in real-world settings and fostering a sense of independence.

Beyond the academic realm, sports played a significant role in my college life. Representing the college in table tennis and occasionally indulging in cricket matches became outlets for physical activity and moments of camaraderie with fellow students.

The enduring bond forged during these formative years is exemplified by the existence of a college group that continues to meet. The strong ties that bind us together transcend the passing of time and geographical distances. These reunions serve as a testament to the lasting friendships formed during our college years, showcasing the depth of connections that extend beyond shared classrooms and academic pursuits.

The journey to college was a daily adventure, a blend of physical activity, camaraderie, and a zest for life. Whether on a bicycle or using public transport, the 17-kilometer commute to and from my house became a routine filled with energy and joy. Even after the rigors of college, the day didn't end without a few rounds of street cricket, the passion for the game propelling us onto the field for a friendly match.

Staying connected with Piyush, a dear friend from school, was a constant in my college routine. Regular visits, shared laughter, and the comfort of a familiar friendship provided a welcome respite from the demands of academic life. In the midst of new experiences, it was grounding to have a friend who shared the nostalgia of school days.

The financial journey through college was supported by a continued scholarship, a lifeline that facilitated my education. Completing studies with the funds received through this scholarship was not just a personal achievement but a testament to the value of accessible education.

The unwavering support of my mother added a layer of warmth and care to the college experience. Whether it was getting up early to share a cup of tea during the morning study sessions or ensuring a proper dinner, her consistent presence was a source of comfort. This continued even during the early days of working for THINK Gas, where late-night returns were met with her concern for a well-balanced meal.

In the academic realm, the focus went beyond individual achievements. It was centered on team building, knowledge sharing, and collective growth. Developing a leadership style that fostered collaboration, and mutual support became a priority. The ethos of growing together became a guiding principle, shaping both academic and personal pursuits.

One memorable excursion took us to the Coca Cola factory, conveniently located near our college. These visits were not just about tasting various products; they provided valuable learning experience on manufacturing processes. The factory tour offered insights into the intricacies of production, and the chance to drink any bottled beverage directly from the carousel added a fun dimension to the learning process.

The college years were not just about academics; they were a mosaic of experiences that encapsulated the spirit of youth, friendship, and personal growth. The daily commute, cricket matches, visits to friends, and cultural celebrations enriched the academic journey, creating a tapestry of memories that continues to resonate. As the journey through college concluded, the bonds formed and the lessons learned laid the foundation for a future where the values of teamwork, learning, and shared experiences would continue to guide the way. The echoes of those college days, filled with simplicity, camaraderie, and the pursuit of knowledge, remain a cherished part of my life's narrative.

The years spent at MREC were more than an academic pursuit; they were a crucible of growth, resilience, and shared experiences. The challenges of language, the adventures of ragging, and the socio-political context of the times all contributed to the rich tapestry of memories that shaped us into the individuals we became upon graduating in late 1981.

After completing our engineering education, each of us pursued our own career paths, but we stayed in touch and made an effort to meet whenever possible to share life stories. In our recent gathering in Nagpur in early 2023, we realized that while each of us had built a successful career and enjoyed fulfilling lives with our families, the competitive spirit of our college days—striving for high grades and success—had faded. Now, the focus is on happiness and contentment, rather than just achieving more.

In 1982, during my tenure at NEI Jaipur, I was fortunate to receive a valuable suggestion from my supervisor, Mr. ML Sharda. He recommended that I join the Jaipur Gulabinagar Jaycee, an organization that would prove instrumental in shaping my professional journey. Little did I know at the time, this decision would not only enhance my managerial skills but also cultivate a host of other essential competencies.

Joining Jaipur Gulabinagar Jaycee opened doors to opportunities for personal and professional growth. It served as a platform for me to hone my managerial skills, refine my resource management abilities, and polish my communication proficiency. Each interaction and engagement within the organization presented a chance for learning and development, propelling me towards becoming a more adept leader and decision-maker.

One of the pivotal moments in my journey with Jaipur Gulabinagar Jaycee occurred when I undertook my first major project on Time Management. With the support and guidance of the Center of Management Studies, Jaipur, I spearheaded the initiative, aiming to delve into the nuances of effective time utilization and productivity enhancement. The project, which commenced on 1st May 1983, marked a significant milestone in my professional trajectory.

Organizing the Time Management project not only bolstered my managerial acumen but also provided a platform to enhance my interpersonal skills. Collaborating with diverse stakeholders, delegating tasks, and fostering teamwork were integral aspects of the project execution process. Through effective communication and coordination, we navigated challenges and achieved our objectives, thereby fortifying my ability to interact and collaborate with individuals from varied backgrounds.

Moreover, my involvement in Jaipur Gulabinagar Jaycee cultivated a spirit of community service and social responsibility within me.

Engaging in philanthropic endeavours and contributing towards the betterment of society instilled a sense of purpose and fulfilment. It underscored the importance of giving back to the community and leveraging one's skills and resources for the greater good.

As I reflect on my journey with Jaipur Gulabinagar Jaycee, I am deeply grateful for the invaluable lessons and experiences it has bestowed upon me. The organization served as a catalyst for personal and professional growth, equipping me with essential skills and competencies that continue to shape my career trajectory to this day. Moreover, the relationships forged, and the camaraderie shared within the organization have left an indelible mark on my life, underscoring the significance of teamwork, collaboration, and collective endeavour.

I had the opportunity to grasp the essence of time, the most valuable and irreplaceable resource, which has had a profound impact on my professional life. Time is unlike any other resource—it cannot be stored like materials or accumulated like money. It cannot be paused or resumed like a machine. Once time is lost, it is truly gone, and with it, a part of our life is lost forever.

> At times, we may find ourselves either underloaded or overloaded, but those who manage time effectively remain in control.

Parkinson's Law wisely observes, "Work expands to fill the time available." This holds true in our daily experiences. Time is constantly spent, whether productively or wastefully, at a fixed rate of 60 minutes per hour.

For every organized individual, mastering time management is crucial. No matter how skilled, capable, or experienced one is, these qualities alone do not guarantee effectiveness. True effectiveness comes from managing time with determination and self-discipline. This applies universally—whether one is a professional, academic, businessperson, homemaker, or belongs to any other walk of life.

"Success in both personal and professional life stems from mastering time management through discipline, determination, and strategic planning. The experiences shared underscore the importance of teamwork, lifelong learning, and giving back to the community while making the most of every moment."

9: Milestones of Resilience and Collaboration

Resilience weaves the threads of shared dreams, bonds, and enduring support.

In the early years of my career, I had the privilege of working with M/s Sanghi, dealers for Kirloskar tractors in Jaipur who were selling Tractors to farmers as well as to institutional customers of Kirloskar make. This stint provided a valuable exposure to rural markets and farmers. The graciousness and cultural richness of the people in the villages left a lasting impression. During our visits, each household insisted we share lunch, emphasizing the warmth and hospitality prevalent in those communities.

My journey continued as I joined NEI, specializing in manufacturing NBC-branded bearings, in February 1982. Working on the shop floor, producing bearings for railway wagons, brought me face-to-face with a diverse workforce, including over 100 workers across three shifts. It was my first encounter with individuals facing challenges in their personal lives yet delivering their best based on their skills. These were simple people confronting difficulties to meet their basic needs.

During this period, my daily routine involved cycling to work and spending nearly 12-14 hours each day. This phase served as a significant learning platform, not only from a technical perspective but also in terms of human interaction. These experiences laid the foundation for facing more substantial challenges in life. Connect this para with page 70. This seems repetitive.

The Management Information System (MIS) was unique, with a single-page report covering the company's functions being sufficient to keep operations streamlined.

Safety protocols were insufficient, with workers handling machines without proper personal protective equipment (PPE). The manuals emphasized the standard operating procedures (SOP), but the reality on the shop floor was sometimes different. Workers were not ready to accept these changes on the shop floor as part of their personal lives because of a lack of resources. The attitude of some workers presented challenges, supported by the strength of the workers' union. Instances of workers leaving early without notice or arriving under the influence of alcohol were not uncommon.

One of the key incidents still lives in my heart. I used to be very thin and decided to dare the system. I picked up the attendance card of one of the workers closer to the union leader who left early without asking permission. The result was that the time office marked him absent for half a day. The union leader next morning approached me and, with a warning, asked me to correct his attendance. Union was very strong, and I did it as I had a plan. It happened again after a few days, and I did the same thing and once again got the request to correct attendance. This happened a few more times, and the cycle was repeated. On one day, I challenged the union leader and asked him to speak to the worker so that he followed the rule book rather than the union leader every time he approached me for correction. I made the point that it is in the interest of workers and unions that productivity and discipline are maintained in the organization. The union leader got the message, and I found that in a few days we had a friendly and disciplined shop floor.

Persuasion and negotiations with the union leader were necessary to rectify these situations. I realized it is important to have a human touch in the profession, whatever work we do. Most of the time will be spent improving the quality of life of our colleagues and workers, and once we are successful in this approach, we will always receive higher productivity and value creation.

There was a prevailing sentiment that, during that period, the private sector prioritized profit-making over creating an ecosystem where workers could enhance their quality of life.

Time has changed now, and a few days ago, I visited this company, NEI, and found it was doing very well and had become modern and worker friendly. We can watch their advertisements on TV promoting NBC bearings as premium-quality next-generation bearings.

It is important that a lot has been learned and changed in the last 50 years, which makes us feel proud.

During the night shift, I found myself with some additional time and began composing poems centered around human relationships. Rajeev Tandon, a colleague at work, was particularly supportive and appreciative of my creative endeavors. It was during this period that I used a portion of my savings to purchase my very first two-wheeler, a Luna manufactured by Kinetic Engineering.

In June 1983, I transitioned to the Indian Oil Corporation with the objective of pursuing a more structured career path. This marked the first time I had left home for an extended period, and the emotional farewell from my family was a poignant moment. Arriving at Bombay Central, I was received by a friend, Sanjay Pandey, who assisted me during the initial days until I found alternative accommodation. He studied with me in college and was doing an MTech. in civil engineering at the Victoria Jubilee Institute of Technology in Mumbai. I also got help from Sanjay Singh Katyal, also from my college who was working with Air India. I had lived with him in his hostel whenever it was required.

The initial six months at Indian Oil Corporation were groundbreaking, involving comprehensive training in various key marketing functions. This period covered dispensing fuel at stations, testing fuel in laboratories, filling fuel in tankers, and various other facets of the petroleum industry. This extensive exposure served as a confidence-builder and a thorough introduction to the petroleum sector. One memorable experience during this time was my first Indian Airlines flight from Mumbai to Bhuj to visit Kandla port.

My journey at Indian Oil Corporation commenced in the LPG function after the Shakurbasti fire in 1983, which was one of the most significant LPG disasters. My role primarily focused on planning the development of LPG infrastructure, emphasizing technology, safety, and efficiency. Subsequently, I transitioned to technical services, providing opportunities to visit industries across diverse sectors, including cement, engineering, chemical, fertilizer, defence, railways, paper, textiles, and steel. Understanding industrial processes and witnessing their growth became a pivotal aspect of my learning curve. Additionally, there was a substantial focus on energy management, leading to the development and sale of energy-efficient lubricants to various industries.

In the bustling city of Mumbai, finding accommodation was a formidable challenge during the early days of my career. As a determined professional, I resorted to staying as a tenant in various government store private. colonies such as Matunga, Santacruz, Kandivali, Andheri, Ville Parle, Kurla, and even Vashi when it was not yet connected by train. The journey was tough, but, as they say, tough times foster resilience. There was no turning back; Mumbai had become my world, and moving forward was the only way.

The struggle for survival in a city known for its fast-paced life and relentless demands taught me invaluable lessons. I recall using an iron to prepare papad or brewing coffee from geyser water, showcasing the adaptability one learns during challenging times. Playing a secondary role in cooking at home, where cleaning utensils became my responsibility to facilitate a colleague's preparation of a decent meal, emphasized the importance of teamwork and mutual support. I met Manoj Mathur while working in Indian Oil, fantastic person in Mumbai and my friendship got extended with his family members during my stay in Bhopal.

> I cherish relationships that have endured for over four to five decades, a testament to the enduring power of shared experiences and needs.

During this period, the profound impact of the word "need" became evident. Establishing needs among people forms the bedrock of strong relationships. Throughout our lives, we encounter numerous individuals, forming connections with them to address our evolving needs. Even when needs evolve or diminish, maintaining connections remains crucial.

Working in a public sector undertaking (PSU) came with its own set of challenges, including relatively modest salaries. Recognizing that a basic engineering degree might not be sufficient for substantial growth, I enrolled in part-time postgraduate diploma courses in systems management and marketing management in 1985 and 1986. These courses, completed at the prestigious Jamnalal Bajaj Institute of Management, provided me with confidence and a comprehensive understanding of the business world. Interacting with students from various sectors enriched my perspective.

During my studies, I had the pleasure of meeting Rajeev Shesh, the son of the renowned Hindi playwright Dr. Shaker Shesh. A group of friends and I decided to stage his famous Hindi play, FANDI. We pooled our money to finance the production and personally sold tickets by inviting our friends and relatives. Hosting the play at the prestigious Patkar Hall in South Mumbai was a memorable experience. While all guests were warmly welcomed, a senior citizen couple received a special red-carpet reception when they arrived to watch our performance after purchasing tickets. It is difficult to earn the admiration of your effort, one must be really good at what they do. Following the event, we celebrated our successful production.

To further enhance my skills, especially in public speaking, I enrolled in a six-month course at the Nazareth Public Speaking Academy. The experience significantly improved my communication skills, reinforcing my belief in continual self-improvement to excel in various facets of life.

During my visit to Vanaz Engineering Pune in 1985-1986, I could see a few blind people operating small drilling machines. This was my first exposure to CSR activities by a corporate company. Any activity to empower handicapped people is really an inspiring event for many corporations and individuals.

Indian Oil Corporation (IOCL) provided unique benefits, including home loans at reduced interest rates, a rarity among banks at that time. The first 10% of the booking amount had to be paid to the builder, a sum that many of us didn't have readily available. During Diwali, colleagues would pool their bonuses to help one of us secure a house. I was fortunate to benefit from this cooperative effort, allowing me to purchase my first home in Kandivali East, spanning approximately 500 sq ft. The camaraderie and support during this time created enduring memories.

"The importance of collaboration, mutual support, and continuous learning is emphasized— through teamwork, educational pursuits, and maintaining lifelong relationships. Ultimately, fostering a human touch in professional life and helping others along the way can lead to success and happiness."

10: Guiding Lights: Life, Business, and Relationships

Guiding lights illuminate paths of resilience, trust, and collaboration.

The year 1989 brought unparalleled joy into our lives as we welcomed our first child, Prashant, on January 28th, in the vibrant city of Mumbai. This momentous occasion marked a new chapter for our family, filled with love and shared responsibilities. Around the same time, my professional journey took me to Bhopal, opening avenues for personal and academic growth.

In Bhopal, I embarked on a Master's in Thermal Engineering programme at Maulana Azad Institute of Technology. This educational pursuit not only deepened my technical understanding but also provided opportunities to engage with premier public sector undertakings (PSUs) like BHEL. During my visits, I crossed paths with Mr. Vijay Joshi, a senior manager at the plant, who would go on to become a cherished friend and a steadfast source of motivation. His dedication to work and passion for the Hindi language left an indelible mark on our professional and personal interactions.

Amit Agarwal, a youthful scholar and our neighbour in Bhopal, hails from a family renowned for their exceptional discipline. Their steadfast commitment to discipline and focus serves as a beacon, illuminating the path to success in life, emphasizing the importance of concentration on the present task at hand.

Bhopal, still recuperating from the aftermath of the Bhopal gas tragedy (the Union Carbide incident), focused on rebuilding with an emphasis on cleanliness, environmental well-being, and an improved quality of life. It was during this period that the HBJ pipeline, a major gas infrastructure project, was under construction. Visits to Jabua, Guna, and Bijaipur compressor stations of GAIL India, along with Petrochemical plants and NFL Guna, provided insights into the vital role of energy in various industrial processes.

Frequent visits to Itarsi, a pivotal location, allowed me to witness the operations at the Itarsi diesel engine shed, a critical component of the Indian Railways. Travelling in a diesel engine was both thrilling and enlightening, offering a firsthand understanding of the meticulous attention, concentration, and presence of mind required by engine drivers.

Exploring defence production units, power plants near Itarsi, and the iconic NEPA paper mills in Nepa Nagar near Khandwa instilled a sense of pride in witnessing establishments contributing significantly to the nation's growth. Tours of textile mills in Gwalior and Indore, Godrej Soap Manufacturing, the Tractor Training Centre in Budni, and visits to renowned facilities like the Vikram cement plant, Lupin Laboratory, and Ipca Laboratory underscored the importance of energy utilization and fuel conservation.

Reflecting on my early days at Indian Oil, I fondly recalled the guidance and leadership of notable figures. GSK Masud, my first boss in the LPG department, exemplified the significance of calmness and honesty in business growth. Interactions with supervisors like Pathan highlighted the importance of aligning job responsibilities with an individual's skill set. Leaders such as BK Bakhshi emphasized the value of knowing people by name and appreciating their contributions, fostering a positive work culture.

I had the opportunity to meet Shreenarayan Agrawal in the late 1980s during my professional life in the energy sector. A very humble and sharp-minded individual, he has always inspired me to have a goal in life and to keep working hard. His mantra is perseverance and continuously exploring the right options to achieve your goals. Even at nearly 70 years of age, he is doing great and is currently setting up a Gau Shala project in Vrindavan.

Returning to Mumbai in 1991, I began working at the Bombay Divisional Office. A pivotal assignment involved collaborating on a prototype to demonstrate the use of compressed natural gas (CNG) in the transport sector. Working alongside institutions like IIP and IGIDR, we successfully implemented this initiative at Parekh Petroleum in December 1991. Gail was represented by Dr. Sarkar in the project. Little did I know that this endeavor would lay the groundwork for my future role in leading a City Gas Distribution (CGD) company. It reinforced the idea that embracing unforeseen opportunities with grace could pave the way for unforeseen challenges.

I also got an opportunity to play for the Indian Oil team in Mumbai and could meet legends like Lala Amarnath, Dilip Sardesai, and BCCI Chairman Raj Singh Dungarpur. I still preserve the simplicity of Dilip Sardesai and the humor of Lala Amarnath. They were the loveliest cricketers I had ever met.

Maharashtra faced a tragedy in the Latur region in 1993 with a massive earthquake, and I got the opportunity to travel to this area and distribute kerosene stoves to the citizens of Latur from Indian Oil Corporation Limited. It has humbled me in dealing with human needs and human relations.

I was also part of the first effort the country has announced to conserve oil by organizing Oil Conservation Week from January 1 to January 10 every year. It started in 1991, and now it has been expanded to a two-week duration. It is organized with the help of PCRA (the Petroleum Conservation Research Association). The objective has been to create awareness to conserve oil by adopting technology and improving processes at the customer end. During this event, programmes were organized with the help of oil companies in an effort to create awareness about the need to save oil.

***

In 1996, I decided to move to the JV company of Indian Oil and Mobil USA, Indo Mobil Private Limited. Mobil has been a pioneer with its Mobil brand of lubricants all over the world. Later, in 1998, Mobil and Exxon—two of the biggest oil companies—announced their merger to be called ExxonMobil.

The Indo Mobil Joint Venture stood out for its uniqueness and ability to attract young talent. Taun left a lasting impression with his thoughtful gestures, such as checking sugar levels on Sunday mornings to plan evening get-togethers. Prateek, known for his storytelling skills and jovial nature, granted me the honour of witnessing his marriage at the registrar's office. Both Taun and Prateek have remained in constant communication over the years, offering invaluable emotional support during various occasions.

> *In the intricate dance of challenges and tasks, the "Take 5" approach emerges as a systematic methodology.*

In the dynamic realm of business, certain approaches and principles act as guiding lights, shaping decisions and actions. This chapter explores a five-step approach, the philosophy of doing things right the first time, and diverse business endeavors illustrating perseverance, strategic planning, and the crucial element of trust.

The **Take 5** program is designed to ensure flawless execution of tasks while preventing unexpected accidents and injuries during operations. It guarantees that everyone involved comprehends the task at hand, possesses the necessary skills to perform it, is equipped with the right tools, and has addressed all potential risks and hazards. The approach encourages individuals to spend five minutes reviewing the task, evaluating the required skills, equipment, and Personal Protective Equipment (PPE), ensuring necessary approvals are in place, and considering emergency management and performance analysis. This structured review enables teams to complete tasks successfully, efficiently, and without errors.

I strongly recommend incorporating the Take 5 approach into our daily lives for greater success. Many of our everyday challenges can be addressed by applying this simple concept.

The five key steps are:

1. **Pause, step back, and think**
2. **Identify hazards and mitigate risks**
3. **Plan ahead**
4. **Evaluate and assess the situation**
5. **Manage and control the process**

Adhering to the principle of doing things right the first time underscores the value of following Standard Operating Procedures (SOP) meticulously. By eliminating errors and ensuring precision, this approach aims to achieve results without the need for corrections or revisions. It highlights the significance of thorough and accurate execution from the outset.

The journey with Tata Motors exemplifies virtues like perseverance, decisive decision-making, unwavering commitment, and going the extra mile. Navigating the complexities of the automotive industry demands resilience, especially in decision-making and commitment to long-term objectives. Going beyond expectations is often the key to success. Dealing with Tata Motors, I faced a crucial moment when asked to provide a product sample. Instead of a special sample from the plant, I opted to deliver a regular product, showcasing ExxonMobil's trust in the quality delivered to the market. This stance impressed the technical head, leading to a meeting with the procurement head. Rather than relying solely on R&D, the strategy of giving samples for testing directly from the market signifies a profound trust in the product. Understanding the market's response firsthand contributes to refining and enhancing the product based on real-world feedback.

***

Marketing is the art of crafting a lasting customer experience, ensuring a continuous supply of products and services. Successful marketing is characterized by value creation and customer recognition. My journey into this realm began in 2002-2003 at ExxonMobil, where I encountered valuable lessons. Tata Motors, a key customer in manufacturing vehicles, was a significant challenge, primarily sourcing from state-owned PSU organizations. Despite the hurdles, my commitment made an impact during visits and product testing.

During the procurement head meeting, focused on pricing, I emphasized the product's benefits and value creation. Despite challenges, I gained approval, sealing the deal even before CEO consent, highlighting the trust in our product. Trusting the product and taking calculated risks proved pivotal.

Another noteworthy experience involved Volvo Construction Equipment (VCE). Collaborating with Athol Lester, a Strategic Alliance Manager, we focused on understanding VCE's network and requirements. This approach allowed us to craft a proposal that added significant value to VCE, leading to a successful, ongoing business relationship. Two decades later, in 2023, I was honored to be part of VCE's celebrations, a testament to the enduring success of our partnership. These experiences underscore the importance of trust, calculated risks, and value creation in the world of marketing.

Securing approvals from industry giants like Maruti and Railways underscores the trust and credibility earned through adherence to quality standards. The rigorous processes involved in obtaining such approvals highlight a commitment to meeting the stringent requirements of renowned entities, a testament to the quality and reliability of the products or services.

Receiving a coin from the Vice President of Exxon signifies the importance of building confidence and trust in professional relationships. Such gestures reinforce belief in capabilities, fostering stronger partnerships and collaborations.

The Mobil 1 marketing programme reflects the necessity of an aggressive drive in promotional activities. In a competitive landscape, strategic and assertive marketing initiatives become instrumental in creating brand awareness and capturing market share.

Embracing safety ahead of time involves implementing measures such as seat belts, compulsory personal protective equipment (PPE), and fog lights. Prioritizing safety not only safeguards employees and assets but also establishes a culture of responsibility and well-being within the organization.

Building a cohesive team involves fostering camaraderie through shared experiences. Whether playing cricket together, enjoying occasional drinks (with the leader acting as a designated driver), or resolving conflicts and then sharing a cup of coffee, these activities contribute to a positive team dynamic.

Recognizing the importance of collaboration and seeking help from peers in challenging situations, such as recovery or payments, emphasizes the strength of unity and the mutual support essential in navigating professional challenges.

The tactile experience of feeling the product, whether by putting a hand in a drum or smelling it, signifies the importance of intimately knowing and connecting with the product. This sensory understanding contributes to a deeper awareness of the product's characteristics and quality.

These strategies and principles serve as pillars in the professional journey, offering insights into effective problem-solving, building lasting relationships, and ensuring a commitment to excellence in every endeavor. Each example underscores the significance of a thoughtful, proactive, and principled approach to business and leadership.

"Success lies in taking calculated risks, fostering meaningful relationships, and adhering to principles like doing things right the first time. **Trust, collaboration, and a focus on value creation are essential for long-term growth and impactful leadership.***"*

Two decades and yet VC invited to felicitate their dealers as a mark of 20 years celebration of strategic relationship.

Raj Singh Dungarpur in the left and forth from the left is the great Lala Amarnath during the match at the Brabourne Stadium, Mumbai.

11: Family Bonds and Personal Triumphs

In family tales, love and empowerment paint a canvas of triumphs, fostering bonds that endure.

In the story of my life, filled with love and precious moments, the chapters about my family shine brightly. It all began amid the rigours of work, a senior colleague, Mr. C. M Sethi who has been Head of Safety, invited me for breakfast, an event that would significantly shape my personal life. Observing me over the years, he was eager for me to meet his daughter. While marriage decisions traditionally involve parents, the visit on December 25, 1986, proved to be pivotal. As the door opened, Kavita, his daughter, greeted us. In that fleeting moment, a decision about her as a life partner was made. We got married on October 4, 1987, in Jaipur, marking the beginning of a new chapter.

Mr. Chandar Mohan Sethi, now my father-in-law, continued to be a guiding light in my life, particularly in matters concerning safety. He possessed a deep love for old Hindi songs and exemplified a balanced approach to life. His wisdom extended to the importance of maintaining connections with both the younger and older generations, emphasizing the value of blending experience with hope. He was always in search of opportunities to embrace life to its fullest. His interactions with his grandchildren were unique; he bestowed upon them unconventional names like Alpha, Beta, Gamma, Theta, and others. With each name, he envisioned a future where they would excel, equipped with extraordinary powers and unmatched skills. His aspirations for them knew no bounds, and he nurtured their potential with unwavering belief and encouragement. Through his playful yet profound gestures, he instilled in them a sense of limitless possibilities, inspiring them to reach for the stars and surpass all expectations.

Through his gentle guidance, I learned the significance of engaging in conversations with individuals of varying ages each day, ensuring a harmonious blend of wisdom and optimism in my journey through life.

His better half, my mother-in-law, Mrs. Indu Sethi has been a very positive and calm woman, she has carried the family with grace and always encouraged other members to do better in life. Her support to in upliftment of my children have been immense.

My wife, Kavita, holds an immensely influential presence in my life. Her impact extends far beyond our home, as wherever she goes, she effortlessly creates a warm and vibrant ecosystem filled with life and friendliness.

Despite the myriad sacrifices she could have made for her own pursuits; Kavita has selflessly dedicated herself to nurturing our family. She has lovingly raised our children and tended to the needs of not only our immediate family but also our parents and extended relatives. Through her boundless love and care, she has seamlessly woven together the fabric of our family, creating a harmonious and loving environment for us all.

The achievements I have attained in life are largely attributed to her unwavering support and tireless efforts within the family and household. Moreover, Kavita has played a pivotal role in my personal growth by encouraging me to learn essential skills such as swimming and improving my communication abilities.

Kavita's influence in my life serves as a constant reminder of the invaluable role she plays in shaping our family's happiness and success.

The journey continued to unfold with dreams, and one significant milestone was the acquisition of my first car, a Maruti painted in a vibrant red hue with the license plate MAS 5575. This cherished possession, priced at Rs 60,000, held a special significance as it fulfilled a childhood dream. What made it even more remarkable was the fact that the car had once belonged to the legendary singer Mahendra Kapoor.

Owning this car brought about a profound sense of satisfaction, symbolizing not just personal growth and achievement but also the realization of aspirations once thought unattainable. It served as a tangible representation of progress, marking a significant step forward in life's journey.

An interesting aspect of this milestone was that I learned to drive from my wife, further highlighting the collaborative nature of our journey. Her guidance and support not only enabled me to master the skill of driving but also strengthened our bond as partners in both life and adventure.

As the years unfolded, Kavita's love for baking became synonymous with warmth and celebration in their household. Her delicious creations not only tantalized their taste buds but also served as a reminder of the love and dedication she poured into every aspect of their lives.

In addition to her nurturing role within the family, Kavita actively contributed to the community, volunteering for various charitable causes. Her altruistic nature endeared her to many, spreading joy and goodwill wherever she went.

Through trials and triumphs, Kavita remained my pillar of strength, her unwavering presence a source of comfort and inspiration. Together, we embarked on a journey filled with love, laughter, and endless possibilities, our hearts intertwined in a tapestry of shared dreams and aspirations.

In Kavita, I found not only a loving wife but also a compassionate friend and guide. Her influence permeated every aspect of their lives, enriching their journey with warmth, laughter, and boundless love.

While I speak about my grandparents, my Father-in-law, and my wife, I would like to speak about a few more people in my life who hold a very special place.

My mother, arriving in Kishangarh village from Delhi after her marriage in 1959, played a pivotal role in shaping my life. Despite transitioning from a bustling metro town to a quieter village, she embraced her new role in the joint family with grace and determination. Her unwavering support for my father and dedication to raising all four children left an indelible mark on our family. One of her greatest strengths lies in her ability to accept reality and work tirelessly to overcome challenges, all while maintaining a positive attitude and instilling hope in us.

Among my siblings, my twin brothers, Rajeev Sanjeev, and sister Geeta, each embody unique qualities that have greatly influenced my life. Rajeev, a practicing CA, exemplifies resilience and determination. Despite facing setbacks in his pursuit of becoming a CA, he remained steadfast in his efforts, eventually achieving success through sheer perseverance. His unwavering commitment to caring for our elders and his daily visits to our parents demonstrate his deep-rooted values of filial piety and respect.

On the other hand, Sanjeev possesses a never-say-die attitude that has inspired me countless times. His ability to bounce back from adversity with greater determination and success is truly admirable. Currently running a small restaurant chain, he exemplifies the importance of resilience and perseverance in achieving one's goals. My sister Geeta is a quite person but a very useful help to guide in human relations and family values.

My brother-in-law, Sushil, stands out for his determination and hard work. He not only provided for his own family but also supported his siblings, showcasing his generosity and compassion.

His love for travel and exploration, coupled with his positive attitude towards life, serves as a reminder of the importance of pursuing one's passions and finding joy in the journey.

My wife's brother, Bunty (Sanjil) is based in USA and has been very helpful and kind to my children. His passion for good food has aligned him with my children. Anyone having good food anywhere makes sure that he/she sends a picture of the dish to tease others, its great fun and binds them together into a strong bond.

From my mother and siblings, I've learned invaluable lessons of resilience, determination, and compassion. Their unwavering support and guidance have shaped me into the person I am today, instilling in me the values of perseverance, empathy, and optimism. Their influence extends beyond mere familial ties, serving as constant sources of inspiration and strength in my journey through life.

***

A special memory is of my son, Prashant, born in Mumbai but we soon moved to Bhopal due to my job at Indian Oil. During his infancy, he found comfort sleeping on my shoulder. In the evenings, he'd sit on my shoulders, guiding me to a nearby toy shop with excitement. These shared adventures became the foundation of our bond.

In Delhi, I attended one of Prashant's parent meetings to check on his progress. Praise from his teacher gave me confidence, allowing me to miss future meetings, with my wife attending. Prashant briefly considered IIT classes but chose to focus on excelling in 12th-grade studies. Surprisingly, on the day of the entrance exam, he decided to confront his fear, marking a turning point in his commitment to personal growth.

My daughter, Eisha, born in Mumbai, shared a unique bond with her brother. Amidst my involvement with Prashant's car work, Eisha would eagerly show off her newly painted nails. She had a habit of placing her favorite frock in my travel bag, ensuring I'd bring back a little something for her. These small gestures reflected her warmth.

Eisha blossomed into a beautiful young girl, forming her identity while staying close to her elder brother. Both children spent quality time with their grandparents, learning valuable life lessons. Encouraging their independence was a priority. I proudly witnessed their journey to post-graduation in the USA, funded through their hard work. This experience instilled confidence and responsibility, shaping them into self-reliant individuals.

As parents, we aimed to nurture empowerment and independence in our children. Their achievements, including completing post-graduation abroad, testify to their dedication. These shared memories create a foundation for a parent-child bond that transcends time, leaving a legacy of love, trust, and mutual growth.

In the collage of our experiences, the threads of family, love, and empowerment weave a tapestry that not only captures our past but also paves the way for our children to thrive as confident, responsible individuals, carrying forward the values instilled in their childhood.

Additionally, there's a special anecdote worth mentioning. Once, by a stroke of serendipity, I crossed paths with Sabeer Bhatia, the Founder of Hotmail. Overwhelmed by the moment, I mustered the courage to request him to write something for my son, Prashant. To my delight, he penned down a profound message: "Prashant – Biggest risk in life is not to take one." It appears Prashant has truly lived up to these expectations, embracing challenges with courage and determination.

Their journey from childhood to adulthood is a testament to their resilience, determination, and the values they carry forward into the world.

In addition to these reflections, I share with you the poetry I wrote for my beloved children. Continuing my passion for writing poems, a hobby cultivated during my earlier career's night shifts, I composed several pieces for significant occasions in my children's lives.

Poem for my son

Sunbeam from the blue sky, make the flowers grow.
And the wind is never tired of
spreading their fragrance to seashores,
We all experience this journey of time.
Where small feet start taking bigger steps,
The river never stops flowing, even if it sees vast sea in front.
It embraces the ocean forever with pride.
You never had a fear of failure.
You have always been a winner in the mind.
It has been a joy ride for you sitting on my shoulder.
You have always made me feel taller than the mountain.

Poem for Daughter

As Sunshine yellow falls on your face
You illuminate with kindness and happiness.
The world gets infinite gifts from your smile.
And you create a world of your own,
Weaving the melody of song

It is a celebration of life!
It is a festival for my darling.

These poems beautifully capture the love, pride, and hope I harbor for my children, Prashant and Eisha, as they navigate the intricate threads of life.

It's always delightful to take a short walk with my father, especially when he accompanies me to buy vegetables in the morning. At eighty-five plus, he remains remarkably sharp, thanks to his daily routine of reading the newspaper and staying updated with the news. His knowledge surpasses that of any other family member, and he inspires us with his energy and approach to life.

Our conversations often revolve around society, country, and the role of politicians. His golden advice to me is rooted in a philosophy of truth and righteousness—urging me not to engage in active politics if I'm unwilling but to stand firmly on the side of what is right. Another crucial lesson from him is to respect individuals with limited resources. He encourages me to speak politely, listen attentively, and extend a helping hand, drawing from our own experiences when resources were scarce.

He often carries smaller denominations of money and provides assistance to those in need, emphasizing the importance of developing a habit of giving. Inspired by this, I have incorporated the practice into my own life, earning respect in my local community. It's not just about monetary contributions; spending time with someone, listening carefully, and understanding their needs can alleviate many challenges in their life.

Encouraged by my father, I dedicate a few minutes to engage with both young children and older individuals, learning about their aspirations and gaining wisdom from their experiences. This balance contributes to making my life richer and more meaningful.

Whenever concerns about the future arise, I find solace in visiting the school bus stop in the morning. Observing children laughing, talking, and radiating happiness fills me with optimism. Their innocence and confidence in shaping their lives with joy and smiles inspire me. Learning from children has become my source of stress relief, and their smiles provide hope that transcends generations.

> *As we navigate life, we absorb values – both good and bad – from our surroundings. Our actions, reflections of these values, contribute to our role in society.*

Respecting hard-earned money is a lesson etched in personal experience – a quarter-rupee coin lost under the bed became a shared effort to retrieve. The value of money, earned through toil and effort, is a sentiment that should be upheld and respected. **(Maternal Grandfather)**

This process of gathering and embodying positive practices is vital for creating a good quality of life. Everyone's journey, unique in its resources and actions, ultimately converges on a common outcome – happiness and a fulfilling existence.

" Har kamaale raa zavaale, har zavaale raa kamaal "

Hindi Translation: इंतिहाई तरक़्क़ी के बाद तनज़्ज़ुल और इंतिहाई तनज़्ज़ुल के बाद तरक़्क़ी शुरू होती है

English Translation:

"Every rise is accompanied by a fall, and every fall is accompanied by a rise."

My father, a reservoir of wisdom, often shared the profound Persian proverb with me: "Har kamaale raa zavaale, har zavaale raa kamaal"—each pinnacle of success carries within it the seeds of decline, and every decline holds the potential for a remarkable ascent. This timeless wisdom became a cornerstone of my understanding, shaping my perspective on life's undulating journey.

My father, the eldest son in the family, worked for Indian Railways and was a great support to my grandfather in raising the family. He always believed—and demonstrated—that simplicity can make life happier and richer, rather than acquiring more material possessions or wealth.

He often reminded us how important it is to spend time together and share honest experiences. Even living together for a short while with a friend can make life more precious and memorable.

This has always inspired me to call up a friend whenever I visit a town, just to explore the possibility of meeting over a cup of tea. It has helped me stay connected with the people I know and admire.

His teachings emphasized the importance of resilience and preparedness for the inevitable ebbs and flows of life. The recognition that success and setbacks are interconnected threads in life's tapestry instilled in me a sense of balance and fortitude. Through this Persian adage, my father not only imparted a cultural gem but also gifted me a resilient mindset—an invaluable asset in navigating the unpredictable twists of my own life's narrative.

"Family members play a pivotal role in our journey. Cherishing time spent with them is essential, as they are the ones who build the strength and integrity needed to navigate life's challenges."

12: Resilient Journeys of Professional and Personal Growth

Every note resonates the melody of resilience, weaving tales of growth and triumph.

Commencing on a journey with Reliance Industries Limited from 2005 to 2010 marked a pivotal phase in my professional expedition, unveiling insights into diverse sectors and fostering valuable connections.

During this period, one notable endeavour was spearheading the railway business to supply fuel, a venture that required a delicate balance between efficiency, regulatory compliance, and customer satisfaction. Taking on a leadership role, I navigated the intricate logistics and operations associated with fuel supply to the railway sector. It was a completely new experience, revealing unique customer mindsets, work cultures, purchasing procedures, and local dynamics unlike those with other customers. To address these challenges, we implemented out-of-the-box solutions, deploying a full team to conduct basic training at Reliance-supplied railway depots on fuel quality and quantity checks. This initiative helped establish our company as customer-centric, laying the foundation for understanding the nuances of the energy supply chain within a large-scale operation.

A significant milestone during my tenure at Reliance was my first exposure to Excel modeling. Collaborating with Ashish Rana on refining the Excel models for the refinery business provided me with a quantitative lens into the intricate financial dynamics of the industry.

It became evident that while an excel sheet may provide guidance, the true outcome is influenced by intuition and expertise. We can meticulously outline procedures akin to writing a book on how to hunt a lion, but anticipating the actual response, especially when faced with the lion's roar, remains unpredictable. Such situations may even cause the gun to slip from the hands of the hunters. Successful hunters, distinguished by their courage and experience, demonstrate the ability to maintain composure and wield the gun effectively in real-life scenarios.

This experience kindled an interest in mergers and acquisitions (M&A), leading me to explore the evaluation of potential M&A opportunities within the market. It was a period of learning and applying financial acumen to strategic decision-making.

Commuting to my workplace demanded a substantial two-hour drive from my home, prompting the idea of carpooling. This initiative not only led to fuel savings but also fostered a sense of camaraderie among fellow commuters. Joining me in this carpooling venture were I.K Das, Utkarsh, and Praveen Jain. Our shared journeys provided ample opportunity for engaging in discussions on various topics. It was during one of these rides that I.K Das proposed the idea of documenting our diverse experiences in a book.

Guiding the vast experience at Reliance Industries, I recognized the importance of leveraging personal and professional networks. Managing interactions within such a colossal organization necessitated a combination of personal connections and professional collaborations. Building on existing relationships with family friends and industry professionals became instrumental in understanding the organizational dynamics and steering initiatives effectively.

Despite Reliance's stature as a giant conglomerate, there was a distinct emphasis on maintaining a human touch in operations. The belief in sending people into the field to carry out work resonated with the core values of hands-on management. This approach not only ensured a ground-level understanding of processes but also fostered a culture of engagement and accountability.

Fueling my passion for the Oil & Gas sector, I expressed an interest in pursuing projects in this domain. However, my aspirations faced initial resistance, with concerns raised about my lack of previous experience in exploration or within a company like ONGC. Despite this setback, my determination to contribute to the Oil & Gas sector remained unwavering.

A turning point materialized when I met officials from the Jay Group, a company recently awarded an oil block in Ahmedabad. This encounter presented a golden opportunity to work with them and spearhead a project in the Oil & Gas sector. Leading this project not only validated my capabilities but also provided a platform to apply my skills and insights to the dynamic landscape of oil exploration and production.

In retrospect, my tenure at Reliance Industries Limited was more than a professional engagement; it was a holistic learning experience. From navigating the intricacies of fuel supply to refining financial models and delving into potential M&A ventures, each facet contributed to my growth as a professional. The emphasis on personal connections, the significance of hands-on management, and the pursuit of passion despite initial setbacks served as invaluable lessons that continue to shape my approach to business and leadership.

***

In the journey of life, the pursuit of higher designations often takes center stage. However, I have come to realize that being a good human being holds far more significance. This chapter delves into the core values that shape not only our professional endeavors but also our approach to life. Designations act as a barrier between people to have transparent and honest and truthful discussions. It has stopped people from being real and innovative.

Business, at its essence, revolves around human capital. In a world increasingly driven by technology and mechanics, it is essential to recognize that the mind, with its intricate complexities, is the true powerhouse. People are not just cogs in a machine; they are the heartbeat of any enterprise. The importance of fostering a workplace culture grounded in human values cannot be overstated.

The values we carry often stem from our upbringing. Yet, the younger generation makes deliberate choices, scrutinizing the values they wish to embrace. As leaders, our responsibility is to empower them, instilling a sense of responsibility for their actions and choices. It is a delicate balance between imparting wisdom and allowing space for individual growth.

In the corporate world, a stark reality surfaces you are not paid for speaking the truth but for managing events far from truth. This paradox closely resonates with Yudhisthira's saying from the Mahabharata, "Aswathama hato hata." It underscores the delicate dance between truth and pragmatism, highlighting the nuanced nature of navigating professional landscapes.

Life, viewed through the lens of competition, often pits individuals against each other. However, a profound truth emerges – no one truly wins or loses. Each person is driven by the pursuit of their needs, transforming along the way. The key lies in competing with oneself, striving to become a better version with each passing challenge. Harnessing one's inherent energy becomes paramount in this journey, charming the world with positivity.

> Living in a world replete with desires and attractions, it becomes imperative to find contentment in both what we possess and what eludes us.

High-level skills are needed to navigate the ecosystems we create, managing success and failures alike. Failures, rather than setbacks, act as catalysts propelling us toward eventual success.

*"The significance of **embracing failures** as opportunities for growth, finding contentment in both possessions and lack of possessions is very important for navigating life's challenge for resilience and grace."*

13: Journey Into the Depths in Oil Exploration

In the depths of ambition's journey, dreams ignited in college echo triumphantly in oil exploration's realization.

Embarking on the adventure of oil exploration with Jay Group was the realization of a long-held desire, which dates to a college project in 1981 on "Oil and Gas Exploration on Land." The choice to go from a corporate behemoth like Reliance to a smaller, but more ambitious, business was not without hurdles. This chapter tells the success story of a relatively young oil exploration team, including the victories, obstacles, and unshakable devotion that drove this ambitious venture.

The canvas for this investigation was Oil Block CB-ONN-2009/8, located in the Cambay Basin near Ahmedabad and encompassing 136 square kilometers. The Cambay Basin, recognized for its petroleum wealth, provided a favorable backdrop for exploration, surrounded by producing fields managed by numerous organizations, each adding to the complicated tapestry of North Cambay.

Oil Block CB-ONN-2009/8 is in the huge Cambay Basin. The region is primarily agricultural, with the Sabarmati River running through the southeast side of the block. Ahmedabad, the district headquarters, is about 35 kilometers to the northeast of the block line, while the next town is Dholka, which is about 5.5 kilometers to the north. There are no records of a national park or animal sanctuary.

Block CB-ONN-2009/8 is unique in the sense that it is surrounded by isolated fields produced by different operators, like Dholka and Tarapur Field, situated at N-E and operated by Joshi Technology and Heramic Oil, respectively, and Ingoli Field towards S-E, which is operated by Gujarat State Petroleum Corporation. Similarly, the reliance-producing field is situated towards the southeast of the block.

With the support of the surrounding oil fields the petroleum system is well established in Block CB-ONN-2009/8. The thick Cambay Shale has been the main hydrocarbon source rock in the Cambay Basin. Kalol formations are organically rich, thermally mature, and have generated oil and gas in commercial quantities. Similarly, the same is true for the Tarapur shale. Also, with the correlation of nearby producing wells, the main reservoir body has been established in the block-weathered trap wash Olpad Formation, with sand and silt within the thick shale body of Cambay shale and silt in the Kalol formation.

The project's early stages included thorough examinations of petroleum systems, made possible by geological insights from the Geological Survey of Canada and data from the Director General of Hydrocarbons. Environmental approval, a critical milestone, was completed with the assistance of expert specialists, ensuring compliance while also addressing local community concerns.

> *Putting together a strong team was critical to the success of our enterprise.*

Seasoned personnel, including a former Director General of Hydrocarbons, were brought on board alongside young and energetic drilling and Geofizyka Torun specialists. What distinguished this company was the possibility it provided individuals could participate in all aspects of exploration, from data analysis to drilling and well testing.

Challenges surfaced on multiple fronts, from villagers' apprehensions during seismic work to managing mud waste during drilling. Commitment to corporate social responsibility (CSR) was demonstrated by investing in local infrastructure, thereby fostering goodwill within the community.

The initial data as acquired from the Directorate General of Hydrocarbons (DGH) indicated that existing blocks have potential in terms of holding significant oil and gas, and there is a need to explore them using advanced techniques, the participation of international agencies and service providers, and hiring highly skilled manpower for the different phases of exploration, i.e., the finalization of suitable prospects for drilling well locations and the testing of wells. Company had decided to start the exploration; therefore, we approached M/s Geofizyka Torun, Canada, with the support of existing block data received from the Directorate General of Hydrocarbons (DGH) to evaluate the petroleum system in block and design for acquiring subsurface seismic image data within block area for commencing the exploration to extract oil and gas within block area.

The Ministry had issued the ToR in July 2011, and with the support of consultant Kadam Envior, we completed the guidelines for carrying out public hearings. Some parts of the block area fall under the Anand District of Gujarat, so we conducted two separate public hearings in the presence of the district magistrate. During This event was conducted in the nominated villages in the presence of the district magistrate. During this meeting, villagers were gathered, and once we had briefed our project, villagers started shouting at us and requesting that the district magistrate not allow us to work due to damages to their fertility of agricultural soil due to the use of explosives for seismic works and mud waste that would be spread during drilling. Also, they were concerned about the damage to crops, Kacha Road, and houses. It was really a major challenge to convince the villagers and government authorities. However, we had ensured villagers that issues would be well taken care of by the company for the disposal of waste during drilling and that compensation for crops would be awarded as per the guidelines of the local authority. The company will also contribute to developing schools and sports for rural children for their betterment in life. The district magistrate also convinced the villagers that, with our suggestion to work for the villagers based on our mutual concessions, the ministry had issued approval for environmental clearance of the block.

Seismic operations, initiated in 2011, encountered hurdles typical of the terrain. Large cracks in the land posed water consumption challenges, prompting a shift to Vibriosis technology. Navigating permitting issues and addressing concerns related to existing physical structures required strategic collaboration with local authorities and stakeholders. We could work with an international company like Geofyzika Torun (GT) for this important technical task. The local coordinator, Mr. Suresh Sharma, has been very helpful in ensuring good cooperation and high-quality work from GT.

GT mobilized its crew and equipment in March 2011, which included a 27-member Polish team and 150 members from India. It was good to see some women working alongside men in oil and gas, especially at drilling locations in oil blocks from Schlumberger and Geofyzika Torun (GT). Gosia and Rafal were their local coordinators and had established high standards while delivering the project.

After conducting the experiments, it was determined that 3 KG of explosives should be charged at a depth of 5 meters below the weathering zone. Five shooting teams were assigned to load a shooting operation with a daily output of 110-120 production. The Sercel 408 UL system was used to record seismic data during operation.

Maintaining quality control throughout seismic activities was critical. In addition to Geofyzika Torun's excellent quality control, we used RPS Energy. A specialized security team was formed to supervise activities, from geophone strings to battery storage, emphasizing the dedication to precision and safety.

The 3D seismic operation involved significant logistical coordination, deploying 80 drilling teams, 30 tractors, and 31 portable rigs. Considering the summer season in the months of April and May, water availability was the main challenge during the drilling operation. Large cracks in the land were constraints for drilling operations, and we required 3-5 tankers per drilling hole. Transportation of water through tankers was carried over a long distance, which caused an increase in cost and time.

Due to issues with water constraints, it was decided to carry out the operation through vibroseis, and an experiment was also implemented. The results were very encouraging, but unfortunately, due to mobilization issues from Barmer, the same could not be deployed. However, with the support of local authorities and Gram Panchyat, we managed the necessary water from nearby sources either through a pond or a large bore for our drilling operation, and in doing so, we saved huge costs as well as the timing of water from nearby sources.

Permitting issues was another challenge, as were the activities we faced throughout the operation. The permission requirement to carry drill holes into farmers' land was a major challenge to completing this project. However, we approached local bodies to get permission to drill holes. But as guidelines, we have to pay the crop compensation to farmers, and the same will be approved through local bodies. As per guidelines, we have to pay crop compensation rates per square meter (INR) to farmers for using their land for carrying out seismic operations, which were already fixed by the Mandi Board for different crops, even though it was really challenging to get approval in terms of managing the local bodies as well as convincing farmers.

However, Operation was further augmented by hiring another subcontractor, and the average drilled hole was increased moderately, but due to intense pressure from farmers to grow rice crops on their land after mid-June, i.e., starting from monsoon season, the average came down to drastically low.

Similarly, we faced challenges for shooting operations due to the railway line crossing within the block area. Similarly, some of us had faced the existing factory, particularly a pharmaceutical company, and water ponds used by villagers, so it was very difficult to carry out the shooting operation. However, we had maintained the safety distance guidelines set by the Director General of Mines and successfully implemented them during the shooting operation near railway tracks.

90% of seismic operations were completed by mid-June 2011, and after that, operations were affected due to the entering monsoon, heavy rains, and floods, which were major challenges to completing 100% of seismic operations. However, we were capable of managing the continuing operation and completed 96% of the block area, and later it was decided to suspend the seismic operation due to water logging on agricultural land. After the completion of the seismic survey, we demarcated the block boundary with support for the installation of permanent markers and displayed the block number and company name.

Collaboration with Western Geco, a subsidiary of Schlumberger, for seismic data processing was a strategic move to ensure high-quality output. Personal involvement from key stakeholders, including the author and Rajeev, underscored the dedication to achieving excellence in every aspect of the operation.

The decision to enlist the expertise of individuals involved in Cairn Energy's successful program, such as Mr. Phill Woods from Oil Finder in Australia, further solidified the strategy. Learning from industry successes and integrating best practices became hallmarks of our approach.

In the pursuit of turning dreams into tangible discoveries, the Oil Block CB-ONN-2009/8 venture into oil exploration unfolded as a captivating saga between 2011 and 2014. The chapter delves into the intricate details of this ambitious endeavor, showcasing the determination, challenges faced, and strategic decisions that shaped this journey into the depths of the Cambay Basin.

The narrative begins with the enlistment of industry experts such as Phil Woods, S. S. Yalamurthy, P. B. Raju, and L. R. Chaudhary, each contributing invaluable insights to the project. Phil Woods, impressed by the quality of data processed by Western Geco, agreed to collaborate, bringing a wealth of experience to the team.

Two promising wells, Kharenti A and PK-3 downdip, emerged as focal points for drilling. The decision-making process involved meticulous considerations, including the geological similarities to producing wells in the Ingoli and Dholka fields. The use of synthetic oil-base mud (SOBM) was proposed to facilitate a smooth flow, particularly in the presence of smectite clay.

The drilling campaign kicked off in 2013, accompanied by the meticulous planning of well designs, validation from Canadian and Polish companies, and the formation of an adept internal team. The land was leased, contracts were efficiently executed, and the foundation was laid for a 750-hp rig rented from Quippo.

The operational helm was held by a dynamic team comprising Rajeev Chaudhary, Rahul Chauhan, Amit Singh, and Ms. Hema. Challenges arose, both operational and non-operational, but the small drilling team adeptly navigated them, showcasing efficiency and safety in the face of adversity.

Noteworthy instances highlighted the team's resourcefulness, such as a drilling superintendent detecting operational issues by hearing rig equipment noise while asleep, averting potential disruptions and cost overruns. Challenges in procuring surface casing accessories due to weather-related delays were ingeniously resolved by seeking assistance from another company in Dholka.

Adverse weather conditions during the monsoon posed further challenges, with heavy mud loss and chemical stock shortages. The team's quick thinking and collaboration with neighboring oil field operators ensured timely access to critical resources, preventing extended downtime.

Optimizing drilling bits for different well sections and managing the usage for subsequent wells demanded precision and strategic planning. The team's adept handling ensured seamless operations without compromising drilling rates.

The climax of this drilling saga arrived when the well reached the target depth. Logging operations, conducted by Halliburton, marked a critical phase, mapping subsurface formations and identifying potential pay zones. Challenges during logging were met with adept solutions, including well scraping and circulation operations.

Well-coring operations, essential for lab testing and analysis, further enriched the data pool. The completion of logging operations paved the way for final casing operations, securing the well and preparing for well perforation and testing.

We faced the heavy mud loss issue in the well in the last section, which is technically called the production casing section. Mud loss is a situation where heavier wellbore mud exerts a pressure greater than the formation or fracture pressure and thus leads to fracturing it, causing the loss of mud. It also occurs when fractured consolidated formations with large vugular cavities are encountered while drilling, which may lead to lost circulation of mud—an uncontrolled flow of whole mud into a formation, sometimes referred to as a "thief zone." Mud loss or lost circulation of mud if couldn't be controlled timely, then it may create subsequent problems and consequences such as non-productive time (time and money loss), sticking of drilling string, formation damage, loss of well control, well instability, and loss of well (loss of lives, environment, and assets).

Thus, the occurrence of mud loss exposes stability and integrity to risk. So, the first preference of our team was to cure the losses and resume good mud circulation. We were facing a very critical time; the infect time was the money at that moment. At one instance, we were running out of chemical stock to plug the mud loss formation. Being a small company, we had a limited contingency over and above the mud requirement for the well. But in that situation, we were running out of material and chemicals to prepare the drilling mud and stop the lost circulation. Mud loss chemical is a special material that is mixed with the drilling to plug the fractured pores of the formation and thus helps with controlling the mud loss and resuming the mud circulation in the wellbore. So, to arrange the material and chemicals to prepare the mud, the team again visited the nearby E&P operators, other fields' contractors, and local suppliers that could arrange or supply the material quickly. This was the second time; we were lucky enough to get the required material and chemicals arranged to prepare the additional desired drilling mud and to control the well mud loss situation.

Although this drilling industry is called or named small and conservative in comparison to other industries, it is the industry where your peer companies are ready to help you out if they can. During the drilling operations, every day could bring you a new challenge. It is the industry where operations demand that you be on your toes always because the loss of money, assets, and lives is linked and starts with a minor negligence.

Our journey during the entire well operation was not limited to just two instances. Every day was a new learning challenge. Not only selecting the right drilling bits for drilling different well sections, optimizing the bit usage and drilling hours was another challenge for the team because of limited contingency; the same bits had to be used for drilling the second well as well. However, the team efficiently managed it and optimized the operations without affecting the drilling rate.

As the first well concluded its drilling phase, the rig was mobilized to the second location at PK-3 Downdip, showcasing strategic optimization. The chapter concludes at a juncture where both wells stand ready for well perforation and testing, anticipating the revelation of the hidden treasures lying beneath the Cambay Basin's surface.

The second phase of the oil exploration journey embarked on a new chapter as the rig was mobilized to the second well. While the team anticipated challenges, strategic planning ensured a safe and time-efficient execution, avoiding last-minute rushes in arranging equipment and materials for the second well.

In July 2013, the spudding of the second well marked a deeper exploration quest, building upon the learnings garnered from the first well's operations. However, a formidable challenge arose when the rig contractor halted operations due to commercial disputes. For a month, operations were suspended, posing a potential risk to the well's integrity. Negotiations ensued, and by divine providence, resolutions were reached, allowing the successful completion of drilling at PK-3 Downdip.

The two-well drilling campaign provided a crucible for the team, which worked tirelessly day and night for approximately three months. This phase set the stage for the subsequent challenge—preparing for well-testing operations. The next six to nine months saw comprehensive analysis of well logs and core samples from both wells, laying the groundwork for well testing operations.

While technical preparations were underway, arranging funds posed a challenge for the shareholders. Simultaneously, the team commenced finalizing well-tested programs and writing tenders' scope of work. Weatherford, Malaysia, was engaged to design a meticulous well testing program, factoring in well logs and cores' intricacies.

The well-testing program's finalization was a collaborative effort with industry experts, including Phil Wood, Zabulka, S.S. Yalamarthy, and P.B. Raju. Tenders were floated, and procurement processes were extended for months until contractors were finalized in the first half of 2014. The critical decision involved hiring a workover rig for testing operations, emphasizing rapid mobilization and cost-effectiveness.

September 2014 witnessed the initiation of workover rig mobilization to the first location, Kharenti-1. Despite its smaller size compared to a drilling rig, the mobilization process was executed smoothly. As equipment and material arrived at the site, the stage was set for well testing operations, anticipating a potential hydrocarbon discovery.

The well testing at Kharenti-1 spanned 22 days, focusing on three pay zones with the help of Schlumberger. The team, hopeful for a discovery, perforated the well and observed for any self-flow of hydrocarbons. When none occurred, conventional processes were employed, leading to the emergence of heavy crude oil at the surface. The elation among the team was palpable as they witnessed the tangible outcome of their relentless efforts.

Reservoir and testing studies were conducted, leading to the notification of testing results and the hydrocarbon discovery to the Directorate General of Hydrocarbons (DGH). Following this, the DGH officially recognized Kharenti-1 as a heavy oil discovery in the Cambay Basin. Based on petrophysical studies, multiple targets pay zones were tested between October 2 and October 15, 2024, during which heavy oil was observed.

The entire journey encapsulates the indomitable spirit of a small team, from the meticulous planning of exploration prospects to drilling operations and the eventual discovery of heavy oil. The campaign stands as an exemplary testament to the adage, "When there is will, there is a way." The profound learnings and sweet memories forged during this expedition enrich the professional careers and lives of all involved.

The contribution of the young team led by Rajeev Chaudhury, were immense. The young team gave new ideas and creativity helped to find new solutions to different challenges which not only saved time and money but also carried out the work efficiently.

This unique campaign by this team distinguishes itself by addressing challenges across seismic survey, drilling, and testing, unlike major companies where many professionals often contribute to a specific activity. The realization that a project initiated in college in 1981 was achieved in 2013 adds a sentimental layer to the triumphs of the team in the realm of oil exploration.

"The journey highlights the importance of perseverance, teamwork, planning, and innovation. The team's dedication and problem-solving skills were crucial in achieving the common goal of discovering oil. This is a case study to inspire individuals to pursue their goals with passion and determination."

The Drilling Team

Members of Drilling Campaign, Rajeev Chowdhury 2nd from Left, Maciej Zalubka and Janusz Danda from Poland.

Halliburton Team

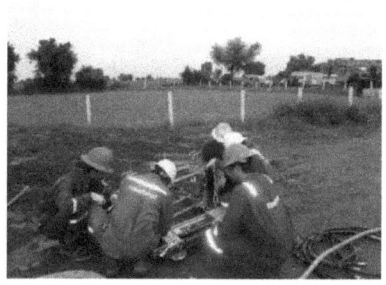

Schlumberger team

Dream come true, what started in 81, got accomplished in 2014.

Geofizyka Torun Team

3D survey with Geofizyka Torun Team

Base Camp for Geofizyka Team

14: The Rise of THINK Gas

In the dawn of ambition, THINK Gas rises, a beacon of innovation, reshaping India's natural gas future.

In December 1991, a trial project was carried out to establish a CNG infrastructure with a cascade, compressor, and dispenser at Indian Oil's Parekh Petroleum Retail Station. I represented IOCL and worked with Dr. Siddhartha Sarkar of Gail India. A representative from the Petroleum Explosives Safety Organization (PESO) went to the site to measure the real distances between the equipment, which included the fuel facility. This has allowed us to further draft OISD 179, the Indian Safety Code for CNG. I never imagined that I would take my first step into the natural gas industry and become a catalyst for change in people's lives.

I got the opportunity to work with Hardip on an oil and gas project in 2017. Hardip Rai is a seasoned professional with experience at Morgan Stanley, Barclays, and UBS. The original attempt to raise cash for oil reserves encountered difficulties. The reality dawned that natural gas was the future, in line with India's ambitious ambition to expand natural gas use in its energy mix from 6% to 15% by 2030. It was believed that there was room for a highly competent private operator in the CGD category, which is currently dominated by PSUs (Public Sector Units) or their joint ventures.

During the discussions we both agreed that why we shall not work together to raise a company in this segment and demonstrate the innovative way of doing business in natural gas world.

In mid-2017, Hardip and I collaborated and began meeting with several private equity investors with the goal of establishing a CGD business. Meeting with investment titans such as Warburg Pincus, Black Stone, Morgan Stanley, KKR, Everstone, and Carlyle sparked interest in existing functioning

businesses. I Squared Capital, a worldwide infrastructure investment company focused on energy and utilities, had an interesting idea. Their prerequisites include bidding assistance, authorized acquisition success, and the establishment of a professional management team.

In the ever-changing energy sector, the THINK Gas enterprise stands out as a tribute to vision, dedication, and the combination of financial savvy and technological skill.

THINK Gas was founded on the values of Trust, Health, Integrity, Nature, and Knowledge. The ambitious aim included not just financial success but also a dedication to operational excellence, speedy development, safety, and exceptional customer service.

This chapter reveals the obstacles faced, milestones attained, and basic beliefs that have shaped THINK Gas into a natural gas industry pioneer.

The THINK Gas story, from its start to becoming a transformational force in the City Gas Distribution (CGD) sector, is one of enthusiasm, tenacity, and a dedication to quality.

Building a team was a pivotal challenge, as industry experts hesitated to join due to uncertainties about winning assets. Vijay Agarwal, a superannuated from MECON, and Mr. Ravindran, former GAIL Director HR, played crucial roles in building a team. A shift in strategy to attract young talent with dreams of making a difference paid dividends, and a team of 12 with diverse expertise took shape. It was not easy to build this small team for the company, which does not have any operating assets. Each candidate was questioned about office, visibility, continuity of the job, payment of salaries, and future roles.

After a lot of effort and persuasion, we were able to find motivated young team members.

Operating initially from the author's house, the team felt the need for a dedicated space. Initial expenses were even made by Hardip and I to support initial activities. A stroke of fortune led them to a 1,000-square-foot office space in Logix Mall, Noida, with a generous owner willing to defer rentals for the first six months.

The Petroleum and Natural Gas Regulatory Board (PNGRB) designated 86 geographical areas (GA) for the 9th round of bidding in mid-2018. The bidding parameters were quite competitive, including the number of homes, the establishment of CNG stations, pipeline infrastructure in inches per kilometer, and pipeline pricing. A penalty system was implemented for failing to complete the minimum work program, and the commercial exclusivity term was set at 8 years with an infrastructure exclusivity of 25 years. Companies with the backing of private equity funds were permitted to compete in the bidding process. Each geographical region was enormous, often encompassing more than one district. THINK Gas has selected 45 GAs, concentrating on areas with current or planned pipelines. Following thorough research, 34 GAs were chosen for on-site visits.

The work climate was positive, with teams focusing on financial modeling and technical validations. While finance teams modeled bids, technical teams went to different regions to validate demand from homes, industries, commercial enterprises, and the transportation sector.

The early days were marked by an unwavering commitment to addressing concerns and mitigating risks. Long hours, often spanning 12 to 16 hours in the office, characterized the team's dedication. Gupta Ji, an ex-GAIL employee, played a pivotal role in managing administrative needs. Tractable and Mott McDonald were enlisted for detailed feasibility reports, and the data pouring in from the field underwent rigorous validation by in-house experts.

The pressure was immense, and the timeline for bidding was tight. Working tirelessly, the team delved into network design, with the experiences of each member proving invaluable. Late-night returns home was met with the comforting words of the author's mother, instilling hope and resilience. Mother used to be awake and make sure that I have dinner even if I return at 3am the way she did while I was in college.

Bidding and Initial Triumphs

The bidding process, a do-or-die effort for the entire team, demanded a realistic and well-thought-out approach. Amidst discussions with I Squared Capital, the team adhered to core values, focusing on customer-centricity, integrity, transparency, environmental responsibility, courage, teamwork, and high expectations.

Twenty-one geographical areas were selected for bidding, with meticulous preparations leading to timely submissions. The nail-biting moments during bid openings saw the team secure four GAs: 1. Begusarai; 2. Ludhiana, excluding areas already authorized; 3. Jagatala, excluding areas already authorized; 4. Bhopal and Rajgarh. Initial triumphs paved the way for the next phase.

With the successful acquisition of GAs, the team embarked on the crucial task of building the company. Ludhiana and Jalandhar GAs were to be operated as a single unit due to their adjacency. Leadership was expanded to include experts in execution and finance.

People from various large companies started joining THINK Gas, and it gave the company dynamism, energy, and experience.

We acquired one GA in western UP-Bagpat in 2019 through the M&A process. We further participated in the 10th round of bidding by PNGRB and got one Ga Shivpuri in 2019. A similar performance was repeated in the 11th round of bidding, where we got one more GA (Kangra and Chamba) in Himachal Pradesh in 2022. Today, THINK Gas is operating in 7 GA's in 5 states and 13 districts, covering over 47,000 sq km of area and touching the lives of 18 million people.

We built a bigger office in the World Trade Tower, Sector 16, Noida, and opted for an open office with cabins only for meetings and conference rooms. The management team was constituted to bring more ideas and to make the organization more efficient and cohesive. The organizational culture allowed even a junior-level colleague to raise an issue and approach any member of the management team. The focus has been to do things right and achieve the highest safety and quality standards.

Sayantan Lahiri and Harsh Agrawal from I Squared Capital have encouraged and guided us to build organizations by introducing technologies and methods that have not been done before by any existing company in the sector. This guiding

principle has made THINK Gas a unique company that has been recognized as the fastest-growing company in the sector.

ISquared Capital ensured that all its member companies, remain motivated, to create value. An annual event called as asset management meeting at Miami; USA have been a great driver to all management teams of the companies. I got the opportunity and fortunate to meet. Global leaders of ISquared capital during these events>

Embracing technology and digitalization from the outset, THINK Gas adopted System Application & Products (SAP), Quality & Construction Management (QCM), and Geographic Information System (GIS), with a special emphasis on safety in CNG transportation with an on-line Journey Management application

(JMA). We introduced many firsts in the sector: reaching households with pre-paid meters, supervisory control and data acquisition (Scada) based on the cloud, introducing high safety standards in CNG station operation, and CNG transportation. Some of the CNG equipment suppliers benefited from our implementation of the highest safety and quality standards in the industry.

The company's core values were defined, highlighting customer focus, integrity, environmental responsibility, courage, teamwork, and high expectations from all stakeholders.

The challenge of designing a logo reflecting commitment, energy, and a customer-centric approach led to the selection of vibrant orange and blue colors. The tagline, "KHUL Ke Saans Lo," crafted with the help of Pulp Strategy, encapsulated the essence of the company.

We introduced two brand Mascots—Money Paji and Bachat Bhopali—to tap into the local flavors of Punjabi and Hindi-speaking audiences. This has helped to increase the reach and market penetration exponentially.

City gas distribution can be divided into two parts. The first part is to create infrastructure for pipelines made of steel for high pressure as well as MDPE (medium density polyethylene) pipelines for low-pressure natural gas and CNG stations. We need to interact with state departments, national highway authorities, the Forest Department for Right of Use (ROU), and other policymakers to make this journey smooth. The other part is the most difficult, which is to bring about change in the minds of people so that they can opt for natural gas as a clean fuel in place of other polluted fuels like diesel, fuel oil, and solid fuels like coal, rice, etc. It is important that we create an ecosystem that helps customers decide on the use of clean fuels.

The team delved into infrastructure development, from designing specifications to tender documents. Collaborations with Oil Marketing Companies (OMC) to set up CNG stations at existing fuel stations were initiated. Prepaid meters offering flexibility for customers were introduced, promoting the vision of converting kitchens into smart kitchens.

Efforts were concentrated on designing compressor and dispenser components, ensuring flawless and efficient operations. The Preet Basant facility, operational since July 2019, exemplified a meticulous approach to safety and operational protocols, with dispenser boys equipped with personal protective equipment (PPE) for safety.

Approaching GAIL for 11 CGS facilities, THINK Gas secured multiple CGS in Punjab and beyond, expediting the penetration of infrastructure. The decision to lay a 170-kilometer pipeline from Rajgarh to Bhopal, along with constructing THINK Gas-branded stations, marked a unique solution. THINK Gas has also set up an LCNG station and has started dispensing LNG. The LCNG station is unique in that it supplies PNG at low pressure to industry and households, high pressure to CNG, and medium pressure to supply natural gas in pipelines.

Additional revenue earnings are planned by selling MOBIL lubricants through THINK Gas-branded stations and introducing geyser installation in households, in addition to encouraging the marketing of PNG stoves in our GA.

Given my previous association with ExxonMobil, it was a natural decision to collaborate with one of the top lubricant brands, Mobil. THINK Gas signed a Memorandum of Understanding (MOU) to offer Mobil lubricants at all THINK Gas-branded stations. This partnership not only enhanced the value of the THINK Gas brand but also created additional revenue opportunities for both the dealer and the company. Utilizing hoardings at THINK Gas stations to promote clean fuel, energy-efficient vehicles, and CNG vehicles by various Original Equipment Manufacturers (OEMs) was an effective strategy.

By March, THINK Gas sold over 400000 scmd gas, with a substantial portion coming from CNG sales and nearly 270 industrial and commercial (I&C) customers. A robust pipeline network of over 4,000 km and readiness for nearly 100,000 household connections showcase the company's rapid growth. Over 100 CNG stations, including 35 THINK Gas-branded stations, contribute to the network. The key focus is to improve the quality of life of the people in these areas and create a good customer experience while using natural gas.

THINK Gas grew from a 12-member due diligence team in 2018 to a workforce of 340 workers by 2023. During the COVID period, the corporation transformed itself, shifting its focus from Environmental, Health, Safety, and Management Systems (EHSMS) to ESG.

THINK Gas outperformed throughout the COVID era by embracing ESG measures. A consolidated call and control center was implemented to improve operational efficiency, safety, and customer attention. The firm went above and beyond, ensuring that contractors offered great facilities for their employees, thus improving THINK Gas's reputation as a socially responsible organization.

The great effort of the THINK Gas team was recognized in the oil and gas sector. We started getting delegations from leading established players like Reliance, Indian Oil, Gujarat Gas, and GAIL to understand our technological steps and operation control. The Federation of Indian Petroleum Industry awarded an award for "Growing CGD Company of the Year 2021, and again, we were recognized for being the Oil & Gas Retailer of the Year 2022. ET Energyworld recognized the organization for excellence in marketing. It was a matter of pride for the THINK Gas brand to stand alongside major brands like IOCL, BPCL, and HPCL in the retail world of fuels.

The THINK Gas story is not just about building a successful CGD company but a testament to resilience, innovation, and a commitment to environmental responsibility. From inception to its current status, the company's journey embodies the spirit of turning challenges into opportunities and shaping the future of the natural gas sector in India.

It was a dream come true to build THINK Gas along with Hardip with the support of I Squared Capital. Life shall be all about creating footprints which may be followed by the younger generation, life shall be sustainable and an example for the future generation to live happily and lead a good quality life. Life shall be: Khul Ke Saans Lo.

"The THINK Gas story is a testament to the power of vision, dedication, and innovation. It demonstrates that with the right team, perseverance, and a focus on customer satisfaction, it is possible to overcome challenges and build a successful and sustainable business. The company's commitment to environmental responsibility and social impact sets a positive example for others in the industry. Ultimately, THINK Gas's journey highlights the importance of embracing change, staying ahead of technological advancements, and always striving to make a positive impact on the quality of lives of people. "A message to the world to reduce pollution and use clean fuel like natural gas – "Khul Ke Saans Lo".

Beginning of THINK Gas

Infrastructure

People & Collaborations

Lighter moments during one asset management meeting at Miami.

Sayantan Lahiri and Harsh Agarwal can be seen from the Global Leadership team from the I Squared

THINK Gas collaboration with ExxonMobil

Mobil Lubricants at all THINK Gas branded Stations

EV Charging Facility

Awards & Recognition

The Company's First's

Inauguration of first CNG station 4th July 2019 at Jalandhar

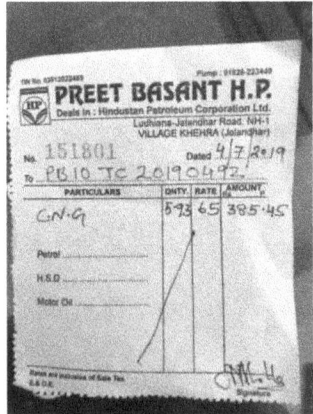

First car filled in inauguration receipt received at THINK Gas

First office at Logix Noida – Puja ceremony

First THINK Gas Branded Station

First THINK Gas branded stations in Baghat, 18th July 2021.

15: The importance of Leadership in one's life

The melody of wisdom guides and shape leaders, and individuals on eternal journeys.

Life is a journey where everyone strives to meet their needs and, in the process, undergoes transformative experiences. It's not about winning or losing but about competing with oneself to become a better person. Each person is endowed with a quantum of energy, and the key lies in managing and even increasing this energy to enhance efficiency. The ability to charm the world with one's energy becomes a crucial aspect of this journey.

In this world of infinite desires, attractions, and tastes, the challenge is not only to enjoy what one has but also to find happiness in what one does not possess. Success and failure are integral parts of this journey, with failures acting as catalysts for eventual success. Managing both success and failure requires a high level of skill, creating an ecosystem where one can thrive and contribute positively to the world.

Our values shape us, dictating the deeds we perform and reflecting in our contributions to mankind. It is essential to gather good and important practices from around the world to create a high quality of life. The focus should be on becoming a good human being rather than relentlessly pursuing higher designations. Ultimately, people value humanity, and this should be the cornerstone of our aspirations.

> A determined attitude toward punctuality can influence the surrounding ecosystem, aiding in maintaining timelines and building confidence and respect.

Wearing beautiful and expensive watches means little if punctuality is not ingrained in our habits. Punctuality is not just a habit; it's an attitude crucial for success. It leads to effective time management and demonstrates respect for others' time.

Time, a unique resource measured universally in hours, minutes, and seconds, is irreplaceable once lost. Time management is the foundation of effective leadership, influencing other resources like manpower, material, and money. A good leader's determination to value time enhances skills and ensures success and values of employees to ensure higher productivity. Businesses in any profession. Actively I worked on a report

Every business fundamentally relies on people. Human capital, rather than tools and financial analyses, is the primary driver of value creation. Management should focus on continually enhancing the skills thrive when they prioritize the well-being and development of their people.

In the modern corporate landscape, ethical considerations often take a backseat as companies find ways to manage lies. The emphasis should shift towards encouraging truth rather than manipulating lies to appear as truth. Upholding ethical values becomes crucial for creating genuine and lasting value in the corporate world.

The debate over the supremacy of values versus knowledge is a perennial one. It's an established fact that values hold greater importance. Knowledge can be acquired, but its application is governed by an individual's value system. Prioritizing candidates with higher values and integrity over those with mere knowledge has been a guiding principle. Values, cultivated early in life, require continuous effort to maintain and practice, proving their significance in the journey of life.

The path to success and fulfillment is not just about achieving milestones or acquiring possessions. It's about competing with oneself, managing time effectively, nurturing human capital, and upholding ethical values. True success lies not just in personal achievements but in contributing positively to the world, becoming a good human being, and prioritizing values over mere knowledge. As we navigate this journey, let us remember that happiness and good living are the ultimate goals, and the choices we make along the way define the quality of our lives.

And as I manage the complexities of leadership and life, I find solace in the enduring wisdom of the ages, reminding me that true success lies not just in achieving goals but in becoming a better version of myself with each passing day.

***

Leadership Lessons from Remarkable Leaders

In my professional journey, I have had the privilege of working alongside exceptional leaders who ascended to the pinnacle of their careers, occupying coveted positions like Chairman in Navratna companies such as IOCL, GAIL, and ONGC. Each of these leaders, including Mr. M A Pathan, Mr. J L Zutsi, Mr. B K Bakshi, Mr. Subir Raha, Mr. R K Narang, and Mr. P K Banerjee, possesses a rare spark and distinctive qualities that have left an indelible mark on my perspective of leadership.

In a recent conversation with one of my leaders, I inquired why he had never displayed anger towards anyone throughout his illustrious career. His response was profound, accompanied by a reassuring smile. He explained that as leaders, it is our responsibility to carefully select colleagues for specific tasks. If a colleague fails to deliver, the fault lies not with them but with the person who entrusted them with the job. This philosophy underlines the importance of understanding the skill levels of those we empower, advocating for empathy over reprimand.

One of my other bosses imparted a valuable lesson when I approached him with a time management challenge. Instead of merely sympathizing, he suggested a proactive approach. By assigning tasks to the colleague causing the follow-up, he ingeniously demonstrated that, much like a fountain needing a balance between atmospheric and water pressure, effective communication requires a strategic equilibrium.

My first department head at IOCL, stood out for his exceptional sharpness in reading situations and communicating effectively. His ability to grasp complexities and convey them with clarity has been a lasting inspiration for me, emphasizing the importance of perceptiveness in leadership.

If we talk about working under a caring leadership, one leader's legacy shines through. His commitment to cleanliness was not a mere administrative duty but a personal mission. Taking rounds to ensure the newly constructed head office remained neat and tidy, he exemplified how leadership involves personal investment in the well-being of the workplace and its members.

One tenure as a leader was marked by a deep love for technology. He played a pivotal role in fostering innovation and technological advancements at Indian Oil. His leadership demonstrated the transformative power of embracing change and driving progress through technological innovation.

Reflecting on my early days at Indian Oil, my first supervisor, was a beacon of calmness, honesty, and hard work. His leadership style inspired an incredible amount of energy, setting a standard for dedication and integrity that shaped my work ethic.

My interactions with former Chief Secretary and Petroleum Secretary Shri H.K Khan, left a lasting impression. A calm and well-connected advisor during oil block exploration, he demonstrated remarkable awareness and alertness to national events. His leadership showcased the importance of staying informed and calm in navigating challenges.

All these leaders, though diverse in their approaches, collectively defined leadership for me. Simplicity, calmness, alertness, and an unwavering human touch were the common threads binding their leadership philosophies. They collectively shaped me into a leader who values fearlessness, focus, and a compassionate approach to problem-solving.

In the mosaic of experiences with these remarkable leaders, I have discovered that true leadership extends beyond authority; it lies in the ability to understand, empower, and inspire others while navigating the complexities of the professional landscape. Each leader, in their unique way, contributed to the foundation of my leadership ethos, molding me into a professional who leads with empathy, determination, and a human touch.

***

Growing up in a middle-class family, the luxury of a separate study room was an unattainable dream. Moreover, the unreliable infrastructure of the country, marked by frequent electrical blackouts, added an extra layer of challenge. However, the pursuit of education persisted, demanding creative solutions to overcome these constraints.

In the reminiscence of my earlier days, the rooftop became my makeshift classroom, shaded by the branches of a Neem tree. The ambiance was complemented by the melodious chirping of parrots and the majestic presence of peacocks, turning my open-air study space into a truly rewarding experience. During this time, the value of adaptability and resilience became apparent.

My journey took an unexpected turn when Mr. D K Tiwari generously allowed me to use his room for studies. His continuous encouragement and unwavering support became a guiding force, inspiring me to excel in my academic pursuits. Many evenings were spent studying at friends' homes, fostering an environment of collaborative learning. During my college years, a friend named Tandon, and I shared a common study space in his newly constructed house, tuning into the radio to create a more vibrant atmosphere.

Economic constraints compelled me to forgo the option of becoming a hosteler. Instead, I opted for public transport or relied on a bicycle, a gift from my cousin. The daily 17-kilometer commute was supplemented by an additional 5 kilometers in the evening for a game of cricket. There were no complaints; instead, it became an adventure to live courageously. Occasionally, I stayed in the hostel for team projects, experiencing the camaraderie that arises from shared challenges.

Each challenge presented its own set of rewards. The experience of working with limited resources taught me the importance of resourcefulness. Seeking cooperation from friends and colleagues became not just a necessity but a valuable skill. Living a cohesive life, rather than a solitary one, emerged as a principal worth cherishing. Despite the constraints, I found joy in the journey, as it became a testament to the strength of the human spirit.

Reflecting on these challenges, I realize that every hurdle was an opportunity for growth. The art of living together, inspiring one another, and building a positive ecosystem became paramount. Challenges, I believe, are not roadblocks but steppingstones to becoming stronger, more cooperative, and ultimately, winners in the journey of life.

In a world where cooperation and support are the threads that weave the fabric of our existence, embracing challenges transforms them from obstacles into catalysts for personal and collective success. It is a reminder that, in the beautiful world of humans, our ability to seek cooperation, offer support, and build a positive ecosystem is what truly defines our journey.

*"The transformative power of adversity, the importance of resilience, adaptability, are the key pillars of growth. The narrative highlights how obstacles can be steppingstones to personal and collective growth, reminding us that our **ability to seek cooperation, offer support, and build a positive ecosystem** defines our journey."*

16: Life's Driving forces

Connecting threads of wisdom, human bonds, and an evolving journey of purpose.

As I am remembering different people who shaped me in my life, there are mysterious figures who appear fleetingly, leaving behind profound messages that shape our destinies or alter our perspectives. These are the Mystery Men, whose brief encounters carry the weight of impactful foresight or invaluable advice, forever etched in the annals of our memories.

Visa and Voices of Fate (1988)

In the year 1988, as I eagerly waited at the US embassy in Mumbai, clutching the golden ticket of a granted visa for pursuing an MBA in the United States, an unforeseen encounter unfolded. Seated in the waiting hall, a stranger initiated a conversation. With a casual greeting, he delved into my plans, and in a moment of unsettling candor, he remarked that I lacked the destined path to America. Shocked, I brushed it aside, assuming it to be a passing comment. However, as fate would have it, days before my departure, familial pressures coerced me to reconsider my journey. Abandoning my American dreams, I stayed back in India, eventually realizing the Mystery Man's foresight. His enigmatic warning, delivered in a brief encounter, guided me to a different life trajectory—one that now fills my heart with contentment and familial bliss.

Traffic Lights and Reflections (Early 2000s)

A poignant lesson learned from a Mumbai taxi driver in the late '90s echoes the importance of preserving the beauty bestowed upon me. His wisdom emphasized the significance of maintaining physical well-being, analogous to the effort required to keep a smiling face. It serves as a reminder that our actions shape not only our internal well-being but also the external perceptions we project.

Fast forward to the early 2000s, a mundane evening stuck in traffic near Bandra brought another mysterious encounter. Exhausted from a hectic day, my tired gaze caught the attention of a taxi driver in the adjacent lane. Unexpectedly, he imparted a lesson that transcended the fleeting nature of the traffic signal. He spoke of the gift of a beautiful face and a smile that we receive at birth, gradually marred by life's burdens and stressors. His words resonated, prompting introspection about the preservation of this divine gift. The traffic light turned green, and the taxi vanished into the urban cacophony. The essence of his message lingered, transforming my outlook on life. From that day forth, I embraced the power of a genuine smile, recognizing it as a divine gift and a source of boundless happiness.

Carrying the God's Gift

The enigmatic messengers, though nameless and transient, left indelible imprints on my journey. Their messages transcended the limits of time and space, shaping the course of my life. The ability to listen to these cryptic voices, to glean wisdom from chance encounters, became a skill, guiding me towards a more fulfilling and meaningful existence.

> *I strive to perpetuate the divine gift of a smile, allowing the child within me to dance freely, a celebration of life's mysterious magic.*

In their ephemeral presence, the Mystery Men gifted me foresight and wisdom, urging me to appreciate the twists of fate and preserve the simplicity and beauty that life bestows upon us. As I carry the lessons learned from these encounters,

The foundation of sustained connections, whether in business or personal life, rests on understanding the essence of human capital. While businesses often measure success in financial terms, the true wealth lies in the people who contribute to its growth. Over the years, I've learned that fostering genuine connections is not merely a professional strategy but a fundamental aspect of being human.

In the fast-paced world of business, where transactions and deals can overshadow personal relationships, it becomes essential to recognize the significance of the human element. Business with a heart, understanding the aspirations and challenges of the workforce, has proven to be a catalyst for enduring relationships. The principle is simple yet profound – happy, engaged employees contribute not just to the success of the organization but also to the fabric of a connected, thriving community.

The linchpin of all these interactions is the mind – a powerhouse capable of shaping perceptions, influencing decisions, and steering the course of connections. Mindfulness in business is not a new concept, but its depth and impact often get underestimated. The ability to empathize, understand diverse perspectives, and respond thoughtfully are attributes that can transform transactions into relationships and colleagues into companions on the journey.

As I travel the landscape of professional and personal connections, I've come to realize that the pursuit of being a better human being takes precedence over the allure of higher designations or material success. The evolving generations, particularly the youth of today, are not merely climbing career ladders; they are crafting a life aligned with their values. As mentors and guides, our role is not to impose our learned wisdom but to empower them to make informed choices, to be responsible stewards of their own destinies.

The solution lies where the problem is. Most of the time, we try to find solutions sitting in a conference room, but experience says the real solution is available where the problem is. We start analyzing various scenarios sitting miles away to find a solution, whereas the local conditions and ecosystem drive the real, good solution. So, the advice is to go to the location where the problem is and resolve the problem with an acceptable solution.

The world has witnessed monumental shifts in technology, communication, and societal norms over these five decades. While some may perceive these changes as challenges, they are, in essence, opportunities to evolve and adapt. The younger generation, often criticized for being too cautious or selective, is, in fact, demonstrating a profound understanding of what is good for them. They navigate life's intricacies with a mindfulness that surpasses our own experiences.

Prioritizing Being a Good Human

In the pursuit of career advancements and societal expectations, the essence of being a good human often takes a back seat. The chapter opens with a poignant reminder that the pursuit of higher designations should not overshadow the importance of embodying human values. The central theme revolves around the idea that genuine connections with people are rooted in human values, forming the bedrock of meaningful relationships.

Business with Human Capital

A reflection on the significance of human capital in the business realm takes center stage. It emphasizes the power of the mind, highlighting that while tools and technologies are essential, they are mere extensions of the human mind's capacity to innovate, create, and lead.

Empowering the Younger Generation

The narrative underscores the younger generation's thoughtful approach to life, making choices aligned with their aspirations. To empower them, we must equip them with the tools to navigate the complexities of life and encourage them to become architects of their own destinies. This involves fostering a sense of responsibility beyond individual success, inspiring them to contribute positively to the larger human experience.

The Philosophy of Winning and Losing

Challenging the binary notions of winning and losing, the chapter unfolds the idea that every individual works to meet their self-created needs, evolving in the process. The emphasis is on self-competition, continuous improvement, and the unique journey each person undertakes to become a different, more efficient individual.

Embracing Success and Failure

A philosophical discourse on the dynamic interplay between success and failure surfaces. Failures are portrayed as catalysts for success, crucial in shaping one's narrative. The chapter underscores the importance of managing both success and failures in the intricate dance of life.

The Evolution of Communication

Tracing the evolution from postcards to smart communication, this chapter takes a reflective journey through the changing landscapes of human connection. It contemplates the paradox of possessing advanced communication tools while grappling with the challenge of maintaining genuine, meaningful interactions. The narrative underscores the timeless truth that the will to communicate holds more significance than the communication tool itself.

In the bygone era, communication took various forms, ranging from carrier pigeons and personal information carriers to postcards, telegrams, faxes, and emails. Today, smartphones and communication apps like WhatsApp and Facebook have ushered in a new era. As someone who has witnessed these transformations,

I recall the days when responsibility meant writing postcards or inland letters to relatives and friends during the initial weeks of the month, eagerly awaiting replies about the well-being of our family by the third or fourth week.

As a young person, maintaining a small diary of contacts and ensuring that I connected with friends in every city I visited was a cherished ritual. Taking time for a cup of coffee and a conversation nurtured relationship over decades. This practice not only enriched my personal life but also contributed significantly to maintaining robust business relationships and networking.

However, the landscape of communication has shifted. While we now have faster and real-time tools like WhatsApp and Telegram, the will to communicate seems to be on the decline. The convenience of digital communication has led to people distancing themselves, often getting absorbed in interactions with acquaintances rather than investing time in deep, meaningful conversations with loved ones. It's disheartening to observe that, despite having thousands of numbers in our mobile phones, our contact lists often resemble commercial databases, with infrequent use in our daily lives.

Even within the confines of our homes, family members find themselves engrossed in chats with distant casual friends rather than engaging with their own relatives. This shift poses a significant challenge to rekindle strong human bonds, the kind that requires time, attention, and genuine care. The narrative highlights the need to address this challenge and emphasizes that a strong human bond can only be cultivated through good, honest communication.

In my personal perspective, prioritizing and nurturing human connections remains a focal point. Although technology plays a crucial role in expediting processes and enhancing efficiency, the human touch in marketing retains its paramount significance. Even in the era of cutting-edge technologies and artificial intelligence, people consistently seek and highly value authentic, human interactions.

This emphasis on human connection becomes a critical aspect in fostering trust, understanding customer needs, and creating a meaningful rapport. The intrinsic value of genuine human connections is paramount, serving as a linchpin for building lasting relationships and ensuring a positive and memorable customer experience, especially in the digital landscape.

While technology provides tools for seamless transactions, it is the human element that adds depth, understanding, and emotional resonance to these interactions. In the dynamic realm of marketing, acknowledging and preserving the importance of genuine human connections not only enhances customer loyalty but also contributes significantly to the overall success and sustainability of business endeavors.

It is important to recognize the enduring importance of human connection amidst the rapid advancements in technology and digitalization. In today's ever-evolving landscape, where AI and data analytics play significant roles, it's crucial not to lose sight of the intrinsic value of genuine, personal interactions. My emphasis on the need for organizations to prioritize customer needs, swiftly address challenges, and build a culture deeply focused on enhancing the customer experience stems from a belief in the enduring power of human relationships. As we navigate the digital era, let's remember that it's not just about the technology we employ but how effectively we use it to fulfill promises, create meaningful connections, and ultimately, ensure customer satisfaction and well-being. Everyone's journey is unique, driven by personal resources, actions, and imbibed values. It highlights the continuous process of learning, evolving, and creating a life of happiness and good living.

"The text emphasizes the enduring significance of human connection in the digital age. It highlights the need to prioritize genuine relationships, understand customer needs, and create a positive customer experience. While technology offers tools for efficiency, the human touch remains crucial for building trust, understanding, and fostering strategic g relationships. It reminds us that success in business and life lies not only in technological advancements but also in cultivating meaningful human interactions."

Path Forward

In human life, it's not just about what we achieve personally, but also about the relationships we build. Looking back at the lessons learned from great mentors, inspiring poets, and mysterious encounters, one thing stands out—the importance of connecting with others.

Leadership, at its core, isn't just about reaching the top of the corporate ladder. It's about genuinely understanding, empowering, and inspiring those around us.

In the professional world, we often face tough ethical decisions. It's essential to remember the values instilled in us by our families—integrity, honesty, and empathy. These timeless principles guide us through the complexities of life, reminding us to do what's right even when it's hard.

Family plays a crucial role in shaping our moral compass. From the love shared around the dinner table to the support given during tough times, our family teaches us the importance of hard work, perseverance, and kindness. They are the foundation upon which our ethical beliefs are built.

Literature and poetry offer us a glimpse into human experience. The verses of poets like Makhan Lal Chaturvedi and Subhadra Kumari Chauhan resonate with themes of triumph and resilience, inspiring us to embrace life's journey with courage and hope. Through their words, we find solace and inspiration.

Sometimes, life presents us with mysterious encounters that leave a lasting impact. These encounters remind us to cherish every moment and embrace the beauty of life's unpredictability. They teach us to appreciate the interconnectedness of all things and find meaning in the fleeting moments.

> *In the end, it's not our achievements or successes that define us, but the love, kindness, and connections we share with others along the way.*

"As we reflect on these lessons, let's carry them forward with gratitude and grace. Let's treasure the connections we've made, uphold the values taught to us by our families, and approach life with an open heart and mind."

Leaders to remember that they are being watched by younger generation every day, leaders should always inspire young minds to do better and do right things always. Youngsters shall be rewarded for being brave, raising issues and being innovative. Basis the below phrases add the vision, how it should be.

I am happy to summarize the events of life in the following phrases of the great poet Ghalib.

There are dangers in waves, in all those crocodiles with their jaws open.

The drop of water goes through many difficulties before it becomes a pearl.

When a drop falls in the river it becomes the river,

When a deed is done well, it becomes the future.

If you cannot see the Ganges in a drop and the planet in the grain of sand, then your eyes are not adult but the eyes of infants.

To the wise, a storm of difficulty maybe a school

The slaps of waves resemble the slaps of master.

The journey continues...Sandeep Trehan

www.ingramcontent.com/pod-product-compliance
Lightning Source LLC
LaVergne TN
LVHW061615070526
838199LV00078B/7294